# Nightclub and Bar Marketing

The Secrets to Succeeding in Today's
Nightlife Business

BY

## Louie La Vella
*a World Authority on Nightlife Marketing*
www.louielavella.com

Legal Disclaimer:

This report has been researched and compiled with the intent to provide information for persons wishing to learn about making a profit from various online resources. Throughout the making of this report, every effort has been made to ensure the highest amount of accuracy and effectiveness for the techniques suggested by the author.

The report may contain contextual as well as typographical mistakes.

None of the information provided in this report constitutes a warranty of any kind nor shall readers of this report rely solely on any such neither information nor advice. All content, products and services are not to be considered as legal, financial, or professional advice and are to be used for personal use and informational purposes only.

This report makes no warranties or guarantees, expressed or implied, as to the results provided by the strategies, techniques, and advice presented in this report. The publishers of this report expressly disclaim any liability arising from any strategies, techniques, and advice presented in this report.

The purpose of this report is to educate and guide.
Neither the publisher nor the author warrant that the information contained within this report is free of omissions or errors and is fully complete. Further more, neither the publisher nor the author shall have responsibility or liability to any entity or person as a result of any loss or damage alleged to be caused or caused indirectly or directly by this report.

No part of this report may be reproduced or transmitted in any shape or form without the written permission from the author. Violators will be prosecuted to the fullest extent of the law.

Dedicated to my loving wife. Who has always supported my late nights and out-of-the-normal work schedule.   @>— —>— —

# TABLE OF CONTENTS

# ABOUT THIS BOOK

## "While things do change (in this industry) this book will stand the test of time…"

This book is a fantastic guide on surviving in the nightlife marketing business. You can read and skip through chapters that fit your current circumstances and also take experience from my Quick Stories (real life events that illustrate each chapter). Building a business in this industry is fun, exciting and can create lucrative income for you. Whether you are the venue owner, manager or event promoter this book is for you.

I wrote this book as an "evergreen" how-to guide. That means that the tips, tools and stories can be used for years to come. Allowing this book to stand the test of time for the most part.

When it comes down to tools and techniques involving social media and digital marketing, I've tried to keep the tips generic enough to withstand the changes. The "marketing 101" so to speak can still translate from platform to platform. However since we know digital marketing will change on a monthly basis not to worry I keep my blog up to date with new tips and changes so you can keep up to date. (PS it's **http://lavel.la**)

I have written many nightlife marketing books on subjects such as Facebook Advertising, Using Hashtags in the Bar Industry and Viral Videos. They are available on Amazon for download so check them out!

# ABOUT ME, YOUR EXPERT

## "I have promoted and consulted venues on weekly events that have produced massive amounts of income."

I have been in the nightlife marketing, consulting, and promotion industry since I was a teenager. At the time of this publication that makes 20 years and counting.

How did I start? In my later high school years our group of friends started to hit the all ages scene (since we were all underage for regular clubs). Of course some had 'fake ID' and were able to get into the normal 'of age' clubs as well. Yes, I was one of those and don't condone it! Moving along.

Even at a young age, at the clubs I was always able to schmooze with the doormen, management, DJs, and other important contacts and get us in past lines etc. I guess it was in my blood to want to know those people. Super smart.

As time went on, my following went from a small circle of close friends to a larger group of people I had just met. All wanted me to come out clubbing with them. Not just because I was fun but because I had the right contacts. I was going to be able to get them past the line and get the VIP treatment. I had something here and this was the start.

A short while later while driving around, a radio ad caught my attention. A small local company was selling VIP Cards that allowed line bypass and no cover at many of the hot spots around our area. Although I didn't need one for myself since I had built some decent connections, I was super intrigued by the business idea and wanted in somehow.

So I picked up the phone and called the company. I wanted to know if I could sell those cards to my friends and take a cut. They loved the idea. They got a 'sales guy' running the streets with a card that cost them $1 to print and were sold for $30. I took $10 per card as commission and was on my way into the nightlife promotions business.

I was doing quite well, but quickly saw an opportunity to expand the VIP Card business to include more clubs. I knew this would be a good way to help me sell more of them. Having more venue selection gave people more reason to buy the card. On top of that, it was a pretty good way for me to get my foot in more doors and connect with more venues.

Worked like a charm. I brought the list of clubs that the card offered from 15 to 45 and with these connections I quickly closed a deal to promote my first party It was at one of the largest and top clubs in North America. Lucky me!

That was a great start and continued through the years with powerful growth within the industry, you can say the rest is history.

I have since won the coveted Promoter of the Year award, produced more than 30 concerts with artists such as LMFAO, Cypress Hill, Steve Aoki, FeFe Dobson, Classified, and more. I've had a great stint in music television, interviewing some of the world's hottest acts including Lady

Gaga, Backstreet Boys, Richard Branson, Tommy Lee, Deadmau5 and more. I have promoted and consulted venues on their own weekly events that have produced massive amounts of income, I have built a nightlife brand that is respected all over, and hold a rolodex of contacts that connects me with power agents, clubs, and a-list artists.

And I have a blast doing it.

# WHY BE A PROMOTER

"… this industry has grown so much in the past few years that Las Vegas is reporting that nightlife revenue is overtaking gambling revenues in the city."

The nightlife business is one of the most exciting businesses in the world. Who wouldn't want to be the life of the party, get in free to major events and parties, drink for free, and best of all make killer money doing it?

One of the most revenue generating industries in the world is entertainment - and nightlife including bars, lounges, nightclubs and promoting concerts is right in the middle of that industry.

In fact this industry has grown so much in the past few years that Las Vegas is reporting that nightlife revenue is starting to overtake gambling revenues in the city. Amazing to comprehend the amount of entertainment money there is to tap into.

Like all businesses, it takes work to build up your brand, clientele, and revenue. However the scalability of the industry (how much you can make and how quickly) is amazing.

QUICK STORY:

Someone starting out in the promotions industry, a sub-promoter (which I will go into more detail in a bit) can quickly make $50-1000 a night doing very basic work. Have a few friends? Facebook page? You can make quick money with zero (or very, very little) costs associated. Your personality and ability to create a following, buzz and spread the word is key.

\*\*\*

# THE PERKS OF BEING A PROMOTER

## "… you become the friend who has the 'coolest job on earth'."

There are so many great perks of being a promoter in the nightlife scene.

• Become the friend with the coolest job on earth
• Get paid to party
• Fairly 'easy' money if you work at it
• Let your creativity go wild
• Be a social butterfly
• Free tickets to concerts
• Meet celebrities
• In the higher end of promoting can make six figures a year
• Work your own hours during the week
• Grow your company quickly

As your parties get bigger and bigger, other promoters will want to come out and party at your events. As you can imagine they will likely contact you to get on your VIP list, and you of course will let them. It's a part of the unwritten promoter code.

Make friends with the other promoters and treat them well. When you have time off and want to check out a hot event, you can be sure that the promoter is going to return the favour treat you like gold as well.

As your name and brand grows you can use this same respect and list of contacts to gain world wide access.

### QUICK STORY

We just got back from an amazing trip to Punta Cana. While down there, the Hard Rock Hotel and Casino had world renowned DJ, Bob Sinclar playing.

Tickets were almost sold out, hard to come by, and expensive! I had a contact in Las Vegas that runs their VIP Bottle Service system so I sent a quick email and was connected to the head promoter at the Hard Rock.

Within a few minutes of emailing, I was on the personal guest list. My wife and I got right past that lineup, in for free, and even enjoyed free drinks!

Connections equal perks.

***

What about the money? Yes, there is some big money to be made in the nightlife industry. At times I have made well over $4000 per weekend on a constant basis and, on average, no less than $2000 per weekend. Those numbers are not for concerts or special events, which can be considerably more. I am talking about your regular local nightclub parties on Friday and Saturday nights.

Special events are another massive money maker. As an example one New Years Eve we sold tickets for $20 per person. The venue and I had a deal to split the profits. DJs cost us $800, food for our midnight buffet cost $2000, and I promoted and sold 800 tickets. Do the math. $20 x 800 people = $16K, minus $2800 in expenses equals $6600 profit each! Huge.

# SO, WHAT IS A PROMOTER?

*"Established promoters have a great following (also known as the 'list' in the industry)."*

A promoter is someone who brings people in to an event. Simple right? Yes... and no.

The promoter may also be the person that comes up with a theme for the night, or the weekly events, or books the act/DJ, basically developing the entire event concept. That is another piece of the pie.

The promoter also needs to advertise and market that concept and in essence 'pack the place'.

Established promoters have a great following (also known as the 'list' in the industry). Their 'list' is one of the most coveted and valuable tools in their arsenal. If you have 2000 followers that typically come out to your parties (maybe not all at once but they have at some point checked out and frequent your events), you have access to a database of potential clientele to bring out to your next event.

Promoters wear so many hats in their day to day routine. From concept development, to media buyer, to flyer designer, to consultant. As you grow, you will be able to outsource much of this work if you wish. Just make sure you get experience in all of it along the way so you can properly manage your team and know what works. With experience you will become an expert in the nightlife scene and gain the knowledge to properly manage your team.

There are different levels of being a promoter; from a sub promoter, to head promoter, to event producer, nightlife consultant, and even growing or working with a large scale event and promotion company (like Ticketmaster or Live Nation that produces some of the major concerts in arenas around the world).

# THE SUB PROMOTER

## "This is your chance to learn the business and make contacts as you start to earn more money."

This is a great place to start if you want to get into the promotion business. A sub promoter joins an established team to help in the marketing of an event.

If you have a group of friends that come out with you on a regular basis try connecting with the promoter of your favorite club or bar. Pitch to him or her that you are looking to get into the promotion business and wondering if he would be interested in bringing you on board as a sub promoter. Let them know you have an established group of friends that come out and would like to start in the business. Offer to bring that group to their party and that you are interested in learning how to grow that list.

Typically, the head promoter is going to want to guarantee that your friends continue to come in and see you are excited about bringing in even more people. Be sure you can deliver.

So this is how it usually works: the head promoter has a deal with the venue that usually includes taking the cover charge at the door and sometimes a percentage of bar sales as well.

As an example, if the head promoter makes $10 per person that comes into the club (plus the percentage of sales on what that person drinks) he is in a good position to bring on sub promoters to help market the event and bring in their own lists.

As a new promoter with zero experience, but a decent network of friends, you may be brought on board to bring that group of friends and current list of people. If the head promoter takes a chance on you be sure to hustle, listen, learn and get that support every week. You will otherwise become a liability and, to put it harshly, a waste of time to work with.

Every person that comes in on your list brings you $2 per person (as an example deal). Your mission is to hand out flyers, email people, use social media and more to get people out. Everyone that comes through because of your work makes you money. This is your chance to learn the business and make contacts as you start to earn more money. Take advantage of the head promoter's knowledge. Think of it as a paid internship.

As you consistently bring in more people and show you are growing? Discuss with the head promoter the possibility of increasing your deal. Don't be too greedy too quick. You want to keep him happy, since there is a wealth of knowledge, connections, and more venues through this promoter. Potentially, you can make up to $5-$8 per head for your large following. If all works out this still gives the promoter a decent piece of the pie plus bar sales and your growing success relieves some pressure from the head promoter's work. You are becoming a great and valued team member.

# WHAT ABOUT AN EVENT PRODUCER?

## "… always manage and stay on top of (your) responsibilities."

Sometimes the promoter is also the event producer. This adds a layer to your job responsibilities. What an event producer does is organize (from top to bottom) all aspects of an event. Depending on how large the event is, you may have hired staff to work under you or outsource some of the needs. This takes management skills.

For example if you are running a Halloween party as the promoter, you are simply asked to market the event and bring in as many people as possible. Sometimes the club takes care of event productions as well and just hires you for promo, but other times you have full event responsibilities.

If you are given the responsibility of event producer, you are also responsible for booking decorations, hiring the DJ/act, sound and lights if anything additional to the nightclub's own in house system is needed, design and printing of marketing materials, hospitality needs if you are having a celebrity at your event (you might need to organize flights, picking them up at the airport, their hotel), and more.

QUICK STORY:

We had a major concert booked for Canada Day. It was an outdoor concert so we had the parking lot all fenced off, a huge stage with light and sound production, and had 2000 tickets sold. The venue said they were going to be responsible for the production aspects and back-line (which is staging, lights, instruments, etc), and I was taking care of the promotion, sales, and the act.

So you can imagine my shock when the band came for rehearsal and we had no drum kit. The venue was under the impression that the band was coming in with their own instruments. It was clearly stated in the technical rider (their list of needs for us to take care of) that they needed a drum set since it wasn't cost effective for them to ship one around. The venue just assumed it wasn't needed. A simple mistake and a simple fix.

I get it, it's only a drum set, just rent one right? Not that easy, it was Canada Day so everything was CLOSED. And do you think the venue had the same level of stress as the promoter/producer (me)? Nope. 'It's your show' is their reply. 'You better get a drum kit'.

This was the responsibility of the venue (as per their deal with me) but of course I wasn't keeping tabs on them - I was busy with the promotions and sales. My mistake.

So after a ton of personal phone calls and favors to any local bands that I knew, or anyone else that they may know, we finally got a hold of that drum set and everything went off smoothly. Huge success. Big money maker.

The lesson here is that you should always be double checking what your team is responsible for and what items you have offloaded or outsourced. Even though the venue said they were completely at fault, they didn't have a solution and in the end didn't care. Like they said, it was my show, my name on the event, and in the end as the event producer, it was MY responsibility to fix their short coming.

\*\*\*

So you can see that adding the event producer responsibilities definitely adds work on top of the promoter's plate. When you agree to terms with staff, team members, and even a venue owner, you be sure to be clear of each person's responsibilities and always manage and stay on top of those responsibilities.

# BEING A BRAND MANAGER FOR THE VENUE

## "If you take on the role of a brand manager ... your job is to make sure the customer experience aligns with the image the club wants to have."

The brand manager for any company is responsible for the public's perception of their product or service. In the nightclub and bar industry a branding expert will take care of the club's name, logo, have a hand in the design and event nights, etc.

If you take on the role of a brand manager, which is quite different from the club promoter, your job is to make sure the customer experience aligns with the image the club wants to have. Example: bringing in a hiphop DJ to perform at a club that plays country music is going against its brand image.

There may be many times along this road that you will be doing way more than you bargained for. It may not be part of the original promoter deal, and you should be charging way more for your services, but do these things anyways. It could help advance your career by getting the experience.

Just be careful to draw the line so that you aren't taken advantage of.

In this scenario I'm talking about helping the brand or image of the venue.

There will always be a time where your ideas, marketing dollars, reputation, and amazing entertainment just can't fix a venue's bad reputation.

Imagine you have the perfect concept for the Friday night event. You have a killer local DJ that is going to play for you, your Facebook page is loaded with local people dying to hit your next weekly event, you have designed the best flyer and poster for the event, a small team of very excited sub promoters are dying to get these flyers out, and the venue is excited and giving you a great deal.

This is going to be huge for you... but... the venue has a bad rep for being dead on Fridays, has been dead for over a year, bartenders don't make any money right now so service isn't exactly great, the venue owners haven't painted the walls in years, and more. Your party is already in a bad position and most likely going to bomb at the start. You don't have much potential to make the killer money you are hoping for and it may even hurt your own brand if you throw a terrible event and push your list to come out.

What are you going to do?

First, I would say you should have done your research. Before setting up a deal with a club, you need to check for these things. Here we are, though, and the deal is done. Maybe you have the excitement for the challenge to revive a dead club with issues. I've done it before. Sometimes it worked out amazingly well and I was a hero promoter! So I can't really blame you for jumping in to the challenge.

To move along, I would suggest you use your power of sales and negotiation to get the owners of the venue to move towards making things fresh and exciting. Even with a new promoter, new concept, and new list, an old dead club may not be salvageable. The owners need to commit to getting people excited again about their place. Other than the costly choice of a full renovation and new name, if they aren't committed, then they may face bankruptcy.

How about an inexpensive paint job? Staff and friends can help out.

Some new lights for the stage and/or dance floor? Rentals are super cheap and you get the best out there.

Maybe they need to replace their bartenders who don't want to buy into the new excitement. Get staff in there who have a fresh following of friends that can help get the place packed.

All of these ideas help change the old brand of the club and throw in some fresh, new excitement. In the end, people's perception of the venue and the events thrown there are going to help or hinder you. The perception of the venue is the brand you are dealing with and may take time fixing, if fixable at all.

On the flip side, if you are at a new hot club, their brand is definitely going to be working for you. This will give you a huge shot at making your event hot right off the start. Keep an eye on the finer details of the venue including staff, security, cleanliness, and management. Always give your feedback when needed.

## QUICK STORY

There was a small lounge in my area that fit only 100 people. It was right down the street from a big college. It had been around for over 7 years and had an amazing run. They even booked some major DJs in there to help their brand as a top electronic music venue.

But the place was dead. Had been for 6 months. I had just won the Promoter of the Year Award, had under my belt one of the biggest clubs in the area with a capacity of over 1000 people packing in the people every Friday and Saturday, clubs all over the area wanted a piece of my promoter abilities. So I got the call. The owner wanted me to help his venue out as well. Only 100 people, should be super easy for me right?

So I went in replaced the DJs, designed all new flyers and developed a great concept for both Friday and Saturday nights. I built up their social media and had several sub promoters flyering the local college and university. We had massive buzz. Our launch weekend we had 5 people.

After 3 months of major promotion, changing DJs, adding new promoters, and putting drink prices to bare bottom prices, still we had virtually nobody coming in.

So what happened?

Well, the venue had tired out. Most clubs have an average lifespan of 5 years and then take a dip. This place was on year seven. Zero renovations, no decent lighting (and was like pulling teeth getting ownership to rent a few decent lights to make it fresh) and had been dead for 6 months. Everyone knew it as the empty club, so my work was cut out for me with no major changes and support.

I should have seen it coming, since the place had a dead brand. It needed renovations and a name change to get going again, or wait out the slow period before coming back into the light.

We threw everything we had at it and absolutely nothing was working. It was time to end our promotion and give the reigns to someone else.

Side note: even with several different promoters since me, it's still the same look, same name, and still empty.

***

# THE NIGHTLIFE CONSULTANT

## "You are no longer the fly-by-night, starter promoter."

Rolling all of the previous services and more into one job description and you have moved beyond promoter and become a Nightlife Consultant. In fact, the more experience you have under your belt, the more knowledge you have. With that experience it is natural that venue owners and management will want to pick your brain and get the most knowledge and services from you.

At this point, your value changes. You are no longer the fly-by-night, starter promoter. You have gained experience and are more valuable. Be sure the venue understands this. Use it to your advantage and call yourself a Nightlife Consultant, rather than just a promoter. In the end, you get a deal with compensation that fits your experience.

QUICK STORY:

One lounge I started promoting was a restaurant by day and wanted to tap into the lucrative nightlife business for Friday and Saturday nights.

They had a fantastic location for the nightlife in a prominent club area with tons of traffic already. Their challenge was two fold, 1. they wanted a more sophisticated crowd than the usual college student traffic around the area and 2. they knew the restaurant business well, but zero about being a club at night.

So I put on my consultant hat, alongside being their head promoter, and gave the owners a large amount of insider information on attracting the mature crowd they were looking for. I offer them simple knowledge on running a nightclub and how to transition from a restaurant at night.

I covered and consulted on everything from the best way to pour the  alcohol, to bottle service concepts and prices, to how to make the room transform from restaurant look to night lounge look.

I had little to do with promoting the club and more to do with passing over my experience to the ownership. In doing so, they quickly learned how to be effective and take on the reigns themselves. This is what it means to be a Nightlife Consultant.

***

# WHAT DO YOU WANT TO BE?

## "You're your own boss."

With the above said, what are you most interested in being? As you can see there are small variations within the promoter industry. Some are more involved than others and some pay more than others. This depends on the deal you can strike as well as with your level of experience and responsibilities.

The great part of this industry is that you can sway from one end of the promotion spectrum to the other as you see fit. As an example, you don't go to school to be a promoter and get stuck at that one job type for the rest of your life. If you want to dive into concerts and different types of event parties, you can! You are able to adjust your role as you see fit for your area, city, and venue.

As with any business you need to plan things out, build your lists, and market properly, but the point of this is that you can do what you want to do. You're your own boss.

So start out by getting your feet wet. Work with another promoter as a sub promoter and get a feel for the business and the market. Start to build up your experience and brand and go off on your own. Then take it up another level and expand.

# YOUR BUSINESS

"You need to look the part, look professional, and have something real to show potential clients."

Are you going to create a brand or business name for yourself or use your personal name?

You need to look the part, look professional, and have something real to show potential clients.

Create a website and purchase a domain name. Be professional! Don't just use a Gmail or Hotmail email. Have a promotioncompany.com site and create a YOURNAME@yourwebsite.com email.

Be consistent and get the Facebook, Twitter, and Instagram handles for your company. Don't just leave them in the bare bones mode. Dress them up with logos, past flyers, and put up a bunch of relevant posts to get the ball rolling. There is nothing wrong with sharing and posting articles on the entertainment or nightlife industry, hot upcoming parties you checked out and loved, or fashion advice. You want the owners to check your page and see if there is action, not a blank 'I'll get it started soon' page.

Develop a logo and business cards for yourself. Places like Fiverr and Vistaprint are fantastic resources and inexpensive. Check the end of this book for a list of full resources.

If you have any experience, whether it be helping to run your college house parties to having real industry experience, use that to your advantage. Make up a one or two-page press kit (kind of like your business resume) with that information on it. Add thumbnails of past flyers and posters in there to spice it up and make it visually pleasing.

Do you want to run your business as a sole proprietorship or a corporation? Both have different advantages and liabilities. Be sure to check your local rules and see what fits best. You can start off small and grow into a large corporation as you get bigger. There are advantages to both so check with an accountant and business professional on your needs.

What about local licensing? I know that in my area of Canada they have a bartender license called Smart Serve. A promoter doesn't need a bartender license, but sometimes it helps having it so you are legally allowed to help out behind the bar and pour drinks in the event the owner needs extra help. Plus, it adds to your nightlife experience to have these little 'badges' on your business resume. Make sure you know about your area's licensing requirements and what you may or may not need.

# KNOW YOUR BUSINESS INSIDE AND OUT

"Apart from knowing your market prices and music trends, you also need to know the entrainment business. "

Your job as a promoter is to keep on top of the business aspects and make sure you are doing the best job you can. The industry really does change often.

Read blogs, follow other promoters and venues on social media, read books, research marketing ideas, and keep learning the insides to the entertainment industry business. Apart from knowing your market prices and music trends, you also need to know the entrainment business.

There will be contracts that need reading and signing, licensing changes that can affect your business, new technologies and platforms that get created, old marketing ways fall out of touch, and new promoters/staff/DJs/bands that come up from nowhere that you may want to hire.

A great example is social media. It has become a major part of marketing in these past few years and has changed the way event producers market their event.

Gone are the days a few thousand flyers and radio ads did the trick. With all of the advertising noise, those don't work exclusively and social media has become the new avenue of promotion. A powerful advertising tool to use, but even within itself it is always changing. You need to keep on top of blogs and other online channels in order to rise above the 'noise' in social media and get your message out. If you don't do it correctly your marketing goes to waste and your event suffers from it.

# KNOW YOUR MARKET INSIDE OUT

## "To be a successful event marketer you need to keep a close eye on so many details around your market."

You need to be sure you look outside of the walls of your venue. So many managers, owners and promoters only look at their own customer base, their own event, and their own style of crowd they have in the club. They are oblivious to what is going around the city and in other establishments.

To be a successful event marketer you need to keep a close eye on so many details around your market.

Things such as what competing establishments are doing:
- music styles
- nights of the week
- drink prices and specials
- type of crowd (age, ratio, music style) going to each venue on each night
- which competing promoters are where
- which competing DJs are where

On top of this competition breakdown you should be well aware of the following economics and demographics in the area:
- university or college city
- unemployment rates

- adjoining cities that could bleed patrons out
- adjoining cities that may have potential customers that would drive inward to support your venue and events
- rising gas and food prices in the area that could affect disposable income

Believe it or not, these details and more can have an impact on whether your event is successful or bomb. Your job is to know your market inside and out so you can properly develop the right concept and then effectively advertise and market that concept to your target customers.

# YOUR TEAM

"Your team should consist of people you trust and people who are on the same thought pattern as you."

There are so many people involved in the promotion of an event and there are also many people involved in the production of the event itself. Find people who are passionate about your event, passionate about the lifestyle, and people you can trust. And then always pay properly and on time.

Here are some of the basic roles:

Sub Promoters
These guys work with you in getting the word out. They call their list, hand out flyers, promote on social media, sell tickets, put up posters, etc. You can pay them a flat rate or per head. A great way to track their performance is to put a code or their name on passes or use affiliate URLs (use a service like www.bit.ly to track clicks) and pay accordingly. Sometimes you can't put a 'per head' value on the hours it takes to put up posters or social media blasts, so a blend of flat rate, free drinks, tickets to your shows and adding the per head rate for bonuses is a great compensation plan.

Ticket Sellers
Used when promoting a one-off event such as a themed party or concert that will have tickets sold instead of cover

charge. Pre ticket sales are very important when gauging the success of the event and the pre sales funds are also used towards the deposits and marketing costs. Sometimes ticket sellers are also your sub promoters and sell like crazy and other times they are simply individuals that don't have time to be a promoter but want to help out by selling 10 tickets to their friends. The best compensation plan is the basic commission per ticket.

If you are looking to push even harder you can create a bonus plan on top of the regular commission. As an example if you offer $1 per ticket sold on level one and can upgrade that to $2 per ticket sold if your seller hits a sales threshold of 100 or more tickets. The added incentive will help get tickets selling and the seller definitely wants to make double the money if they have the chance. Why make $98 on 98 tickets when you can make $200 on 100 tickets. Give them incentives.

Entertainment (DJ/Band/MC)
You need the right entertainment to make your event vision a reality. Whether it is a big band, DJ concert or a local residency night, your event concept and who you are going to promote to will only succeed if the entertainment is chosen correctly. Your job is to develop the concept and promote. The entertainment has the job of keeping the customers happy, excited and entertained. If you miss on the atmosphere and music, no one will talk about the event, they won't trust your judgement and that makes it so much harder to get support for your next one.

List Builders
The list building team specifically works on building your following. These members of your team may double as sub-promoters or social media ambassadors as well. They post

links to VIP and bottle service forms, post contests and giveaways, and could even interact at your event and get emails and followers. They usually get paid a flat rate.

Social Media Ambassadors
What a great way to use 'influencers'. These are people that come out to your events or even similar styled local events and have a large following on social media. These are go-to guys and girls that seem to be making the decisions for their group of friends on where to go out. Make these people your ambassadors. Zero pressure to sell tickets, no pressure to build weekly guest lists or book bottle service booths, zero worries at all.

What you need them to do is just talk about the event on Facebook, Twitter and Instagram. Share the event flyers and images, take some pics of themselves having a blast at the event and post them. Check-in on Facebook and Foursquare. Tell their friends they are going to party at your spot and, in return, influence their friends decisions. In return you treat them like VIPs - line by pass, a few free drinks, access to super cheap or free tickets to concerts, etc.

Most ambassadors just want to be a part of the excitement in some way, feel special, and have a super simple job. They may not even require any monetary compensation. Be up front with the job responsibilities and the non paying compensation so everyone is aware and on the same page. You don't want them to expect a weekly pay check if you are not offering it and then bad mouth your event on social media.

Cover Charge Person
This girl or guy will be positioned at the entrance of the venue taking in cash for the cover charge or ticket sales.

Definitely someone you have to trust so please hire carefully and have systems in place that keeps an eye on the cash. I have had to fire many cover girls in my career that were caught stealing from the till. I can't stress enough that you need to keep an eye on the cash. Make a proper tally system so that people through the door, whether they are paid or free or half price, are all accounted for and the numbers line up. Pay well, which could give better reason for them to stay honest and not lose the job.

VIP Host
The VIP Host will usually flow from the front door to the inside of the club. Some venues have a separate VIP entrance and will have the host placed there. Wherever the person is, the main goal is to hold the guest list and bottle service reservations in hand. These are the customers that have taken the time to book VIP in advance and should be treated as VIPs. The host shows them into the club and to their table. You want the VIP line to run smoothly so the customer enjoys the service and returns again and again. There are times that the VIP line is almost as long as the regular line, so be sure the host is super courteous and appreciative.

Security - Front Door
Much like the VIP Host, the Front Door security is a big part of your front line. While they are a part of the security team, we need to remember that they are usually the first person that a customer interacts with at the venue. You really need to be sure their customer service skills are up to par and know how to properly reject patrons for dress code, over-intoxication, fighting, or even underage attempts. Unless they need to get more aggressive with violent situations, in most circumstances they need to let the patron down easily and send them on their way. You never know who you are talking to.

Your team should consist of people you trust and people who are on the same thought pattern as you. If you have a piece of the team that does not believe in your abilities, your event, or your music, things can go sour quickly. Sometimes not having their heart in the right place can create a situation that lacks care and excitement and sub-consciously sabotages your efforts. Be respectful and on good terms with your team. They are super important and as they say "Good help is hard to find".

QUICK STORY:

One of the scariest jobs to fill is the cover girl (or guy) position. This person takes in the ticket or cover charge money and watches over it until the end of the night, when you count it and hopefully numbers add up. (PS they almost never do).

On several occasions, I have had to fire my door person. People whom I had trusted and had no reason to think they would steal from me.

On one occasion my sub-promoter was filling in for the cover girl that had called in sick. While I thought he was trust worthy since he was working with me as a promoter we found out quickly how sneaky he was. At the cash register he would cup large bills in the palm of his hand while making the transaction and giving change. He made it look like it was going into the register and then a second later went into his pocket for his phone. To the naked eye everything looked innocent. However his theft was caught on camera by the management during the night and I was quickly notified. I went into the office and watched the footage. Saw him take three large bills as well as a doorman's phone. When we called him out on the allegations he denied it all even though we saw him and showed him the camera footage. He quickly changed his story to 'I was drunk' (drinking water all night, we knew he wasn't intoxicated). He was fired on the spot and even banned from several bars that I was working with.

Unfortunately, with access to large amounts of cash in front of them, some people see the opportunity to steal and their morals break down.

Always have systems in place to watch over your money till. Cameras, a second host at the front, telling security to secretly keep an eye on counts and the hands of the cover girl, etc. Even then sometimes things slip.

One of the systems I added was to check on the customer count every hour and at the same time remove the large cash from the till to the safe (20's and 50's). This way I was on top of how many people were in and how much money was collected at that time. Being a bit more on top of the money gave a strong impression that I was watching and knew the counts on a consistent basis through the night. Leaving smaller chances for theft.

So many times you get busy with your duties that you leave the money to the end and it can lead to a free for all.

***

# DIFFERENT GROUPS OF PROMOTERS

## "Each group has a role to play in promotion."

There are a few different types of promoters that can be used in order to market your events. Each group has a role to play in promotion. Image Promoters, Filler Promoters and Mass Event Promoters. Your team members can fill any or all of these groups but it is important to have them covered.

Image Promoters
These promoters build a list of only good looking people. They are to target groups of customers that have the right image. Models, actresses, popular beautiful trend setters. Seventy percent of their market should be girls. The cliche has always been fill a bar with females and the guys will come. It is true and the job of this group of promoters is to invite and promote to mostly females. With business cards in hand and their smartphone loaded up with Twitter and Facebook followers, the Image Promoters invite, follow, and message every day.

Filler Promoters
These promoters target everyone by demographic. No need to target females only or good looking people, they just need to be sure their focus is on the right music or event style. The

job of the Filler Promoter is to get groups of people to the venue early. Birthday parties, stags, bachelorette groups and more. Typically many people walk into a club around 11:30/12 midnight so it is always beneficial to already have a room filled with people in it.

Mass Event Promoters

Much like filler promoters, this is the part of your team that goes wide with their promotion. Usually they have large lists of people and don't necessarily target by group. Their primary objective is to get the word out to the masses by all means necessary. A good way to think of the Mass Promoter is to think of a radio station. You place ads on the radio everyday promoting your event. The ads are not targeting birthday groups or models, they are targeting a wide audience and help bring in the largest amount of people possible. Mass promoters may flyer parking lots, advertise on social media or traditional means like radio, and put posters up on light poles. They do blanket marketing across any platform.

# BE OR HIRE A GREAT HOST

"Everyone wants to be a part of the 'in crowd' and making them feel like they know the promoter is huge for them."

Like I mentioned earlier if you are the host, or hired a host to work for you, make sure your customers have the impression that they are all VIPs.

Whether they are bottle service clients, regulars, large groups, new people, whoever, reach out to as many as you can and connect with them. Everyone wants to be a part of the 'in crowd' and making them feel like they know the promoter is huge for them.

Use your bar tab, if you have one at the venue, and offer a round of complimentary shots or drinks for people. Make the large spenders super happy by always giving them the attention they crave.

I cannot count the number of times those people were buying me drinks in appreciation of their treatment. This saved the bar tab and also showed how powerful my brand was getting. Even if you are having a few shots with regulars, never get drunk yourself. Remember: you are still working. Even if the managers don't care what you do, you have a brand to uphold for yourself. No one likes a sloppy drunk person, especially an unprofessional event host or promoter.

QUICK STORY

Many years ago I was nightclub host at a student friendly bar. My job duties included emceeing with the DJ, making bar and birthday announcements and mingling with the crowd.

At the beginning of the evening the owner of the bar came up to me and moved my attention to a group of girls. They had come in to celebrate one a birthday. I went over to the group, said a Happy Birthday to the lucky girl, and offered to buy them all a round of shots.

To make a long story short that evening I met the birthday girl and what was to become my wife of almost ten years (as of this publication). What a host!

\*\*\*

# WHERE DO YOU FIND PROMOTERS?

## "A great way to meet and interview several candidates is to have a job fair."

There are several ways to find and hire promoters for your team. Like any job, you can post want ads on websites like Monster, Craigslist, Kijiji, and others. You should also post the listing on your social media pages and venue websites.

Job listings from local universities and colleges are also a perfect spot to find local, social promoters to join your team. They would be a great asset since they are on campus and have access to students that you may not normally have immediate access to.

A great way to meet and interview several candidates is to have a job fair. Promote the fact that you are looking for several promoter positions and have them all come to the venue with a resume in hand at one time. Pick an afternoon and advertise that it is a drop-in. The interviews are first come first serve and you get through as many as possible. This also gives potential hires a chance to check out the venue and talk to you about your events. Whether you hire them or not, there could be some small residual marketing from them talking amongst their group of friends.

Another great way to find promoters is by networking during your event nights. As a promoter yourself you are always mingling through the crowd, shaking hands, meeting people, etc. Find those great personable people with a large group of friends or access to the right crowd at work, school, or other influential groups and ask if they'd be interested in making money while partying. I'm sure you will almost always get an excited YES.

When you hire your promoters be aware that they are always excited for such a cool job, but not all of them realize the work involved in this type of position. So many new promoters think the job is a come-in-and-drink-for-free type of job. It takes creativity, time during the week, and dedication to go out and invite people to a venue.

When they find that there is work involved, and if compensated by number of heads, you can imagine how quick your promoters fall off your roster.

Not to worry though, filter through the good and bad and what you are left with is a great team. Pay and treat them well and your nights will grow nicely.

# OUTSOURCING

## "Nowadays you can pretty much pass the work over to anyone, anywhere."

There are so many ways you can take the pressure off of you and load it onto your team. Your team does not even have to be local people. Using the internet and some amazing websites gives you the chance to hire people from anywhere around the world to do some lucrative jobs. This is called outsourcing. I've included a list of these resources at the end of this book.

QUICK STORY

I was super busy creating a brand new concept for a nightclub. I hadn't built a local team for the place yet, so I was short staffed and basically working on my own in the planning stages.

I was designing flyers, posters, logos, revamping the venue's Facebook and Twitter pages, adding their information to my own website and social media avenues, and so much more.

On top of all this, I made the mistake of offering more than I could handle. They wanted their lunch menu redone. I did such a great job with the flyers design that they wanted a similar cool look for their menu.

I wasn't making any added money on this menu design, nor did I have any time for it. It was just on the back burner and wasn't getting done.

So I outsourced. I went to the website Fiverr, which is an online market place that hosts thousands of people offering quick services. These people post 'gigs' which are services they will do for only $5. I did a quick search, found a ton of graphic designers that were willing to design a one page flyer, poster, menu, whatever, so I hired one.

I emailed my designer the venue logo, description of food, some images, and guidance on how it should look and 48 hours and $5 later I had my menu designed.

The owners loved it and I didn't do a thing.

***

When planning to delegate tasks, you want to be sure you have a good grasp on what should be outsourced. Nowadays you can pretty much pass the work over to anyone, anywhere. However, sometimes an outsourced person doesn't get the local flavor and those things are better left done personally or by your own local team.

Don't discount the ability to outsource jobs. Some of these include graphic designers for flyers or logos, DJ drops, website and mobile app programming, creative writing, social media marketers, virtual assistants to gather information or send emails on your behalf, and more.

Apart from the example above using Fiverr, there are other sites as well that can connect you with assistants, designers, programmers and more. eLance, ODesk and Freelancer dot com are all great.

I have used them all and built a strong online outsource team. I now stick with these as my go-to assistants from Fiverr and eLance.

# PARTNERING WITH OTHER PROMOTERS ON EVENTS

## "… splitting risk sometimes outweighs taking 100% of the potential profits."

There are some great advantages to partnering with other promoter teams or companies on events. The first advantage and most obvious is the exponential marketing power and network that your event will have. Two heads are definitely better than one and having the ability to tap into other lists and networks gives your event a much greater chance of being a great success.

Another advantage to the partnering aspect is to keep the competition at bay. What I mean by that is it keeps other promoters from competing with you on a particular weekend or event timeframe.

With partners you are also going to share the up-front investment and total risk. If you have an event that will cost you $20,000 to produce, you are now sharing that risk and cost of the event with others. While the profits are also split up, in a rocky economy splitting risk sometimes outweighs taking 100% of the potential profits.

So when is a great time to partner with other promoters? Like I mentioned, large events with large investment and risk. You really want to weigh out the advantages of taking 100% profit but all the risk. Many times you will find that splitting up your risk is best. With large scale events you will also want the added promotional power to make it a success.

Another reason to partner with other promoters is for tapping into a market that you do not have full access to. An example could be if you have a large rock list but want to overlap with the student market and promote a very large student event. You probably want to partner with student promoters that throw Frosh Week parties etc. and use their network to get the word out and overlap your existing list.

# SELLING OTHER PROMOTER'S TICKETS

## "I am often approached by other promoters and asked to help them sell their tickets and push their event."

Here is a great tip on making great money and helping out fellow promoters at the same time.

As you grow as a promoter you will build a large following. These are people who want to come and experience your weekly or one-off events. This can be very valuable to yourself and other promoters and can be used to your advantage even when you don't have a venue or event of your own to work with.

I am often approached by other promoters and asked to help them sell their tickets and push their event. There is nothing wrong with selling tickets to their event, especially when it fits your style and following. Negotiate a cut of the ticket sales, even a presenting logo on their marketing materials. Promote away, sell and collect. Why not make some extra cash during the down time and get some exposure for your company while they are doing the heavy lifting?

Make sure you choose events that would fit your demographic of followers. It can hurt your reputation if you are pushing a Country event to your Electronic music fans. They may wonder when you lost your marbles and even stop following you on email and social media. Don't lose them! Keeping within your brand makes the sale easier for you.

Some tips. Work with promoters you trust. Don't get caught helping events and handing in the ticket money only to find that the promoter can't afford or does not want to pay you the agreed commission. Just as important, be sure you are promoting events that are not going to compete with your own upcoming events. Customers only have so much money to spread around so make sure that your own event is a success.

I even have a Ticketmaster account, since I have done some high profile events. This is something that very few small to medium sized promoters have access to. Just the organic Ticketmaster search traffic alone helps me sell tickets. Many times I set an agreement with a promoter to sell using my account. I create a new event and sell exclusively from there. I receive the money in my own bank account and pay out the difference between the ticket sales minus my cut. The promoter gets great exposure on Ticketmaster and also gets hundreds more in ticket sales that they would never have had access to.

QUICK STORY:

A promoter friend of mine booked a very well known, award-winning rap artist for a concert. He had all his promotional efforts in line that included posters, flyers, radio, street team, hard ticket sales and retail location support, among other things.

He approached me and asked if I wanted to help sell some tickets. I had also booked this artist before and did very well, so my following was a perfect fit. Of course I was happy to help.

I sold the tickets online using my Ticketmaster account. This was purely online marketing and sales with no in-person meetings for ticket pick-ups and thus no hard tickets to keep track of.

I promoted on my Facebook and Twitter accounts periodically and had decent traffic from the Ticketmaster account. With a major tour going on, there were many people just blindly searching the artist name on Google and Ticketmaster and wondering when he is coming to town. Guess which ticket page they landed on.

At the end of the event he had 600 people at the concert and of those, over 450 tickets were sold myself. An act aligned with the right following brought me $4 a ticket in commission. No event co-ordination whatsoever, no $10K investment for artist deposits, no risk at all. Yet I walked away with $1800.

***

# KEEP YOUR FELLOW PROMOTERS CLOSE TO YOU

## "Never hand out flyers or tickets inside a competing club."

You definitely want to know what is going on around your market. With simple research into fellow promoter's social media pages and being added to their lists you can be sure that you will be in the know when things are happening.

Never hand out flyers or tickets inside a competing club. That is simply malicious marketing and it never sits well in the industry. It's just plain dirty. You should set a standard in the area and have the competition perceive that you are all on the same side for the health of the nightlife scene. You don't want other promoters to purposely book overlapping dates and events in an effort to put you out of business.

The old saying "keep your friends close and enemies closer" can be true in this business, but in all seriousness you definitely need to try to stay on great terms with everyone in the industry. You never know when working with another promoter or venue makes perfect business sense.

QUICK STORY:

During one of our summer promotions I had a small venue in a section of the city that was home to about 6-8 bars. The bar I was looking after was tiny, about 100 person capacity, while the other bars were so much bigger, fitting anywhere from 400 to 2000 people each.

I had worked in the city for awhile. I got to know all of the promoters, head doormen and owners of every bar in town, so I had a great relationship with everyone.

Even though I was in direct competition with them all year round, and even had events that landed on their own busy nights, I was still in good terms with them. I visited them all the time, shook hands, talked shop and kept my 'nice guy/professional' persona.

All summer long I was able to take a break from the small venue each night, as it was easy to run itself and I was able to bar hop. I was passing each large lineup and getting free drinks from the other owners. This was important because I was able to keep my face and brand in front of thousands of customers through the summer, even though my venue was tiny and had access to only 100. I didn't want to look like I disappeared for the summer and with this constant bar hopping I was very active in the area. In fact, many customers thought I was the head promoter for all 8 bars! Great branding.

Plus, there were several dates where I was hired by these competing bars to do special appearances and one-offs. With the limited revenue I had made from the small bar all summer, these added events gave me the opportunity to generate larger amounts of revenue through the season.

***

Sometimes having close connections with your competition simply gives you VIP access to their spots, or opportunities to promote events there. Other times it creates enough respect to keep them from trying to hurt your business.

The last thing you want is another venue or promoter try to book stronger acts or events on your nights in order to steal your successful clientele. Some people are fickle and run to the next big thing. You want to befriend these promoters so they think twice before being malicious like that.

# STOLEN IDEAS. WATCH WHAT YOU SHARE.

"Nothing bugs me more than having an amazing idea, sharing it with someone and then seeing the flyer for it come out a few weeks later by another promoter."

This happens every day in every industry. The nightlife and event promoting business is not the only industry where ideas can get stolen.

There will be many times when you are talking out loud to customers and fellow owners or promoters to test good versus bad ideas. This is perfectly normal and needed. You do have to make sure your ideas are going to work before investing money and time. The unfortunate part about brainstorming your future promotions is the obvious pitfall that they are out in the open for owners or promoters to steal.

Nothing bugs me more than having an amazing idea, sharing it with someone and then seeing the flyer for it come out a few weeks later by another promoter. That was MY IDEA! Even worse than the stolen idea is when the promoter doesn't even execute it properly and it flops. What a waste. Even if you had all of the right ideas and plan of execution to do it properly, you feel like you can't move ahead and do the event as well since *you* will be seen as the 'idea stealer.'

So what can you do? Only share ideas with trusted people, including just your team members. If you think it is a strong concept and want to gather more market research by talking to others, you should spend some time and a small amount of money to obtain the domain name for your concept, have flyers designed, DJs in discussion with, etc. before sharing any ideas. This way the person on the other side of the conversation sees that you are deep into the planning stages and the concept wouldn't be worth their time to steal.

QUICK STORY:

This has happened to me many times. Most of those times the promoter flopped on the event because of either lack of promotion or they didn't put the right details into the event and it sucked.

I can share story over story here but instead here is my tip: it happens, move on, keep an eye on those shady promoters for the future, get up and do another event.

***

# TOOLS OF THE TRADE: OFFLINE

"… since no one else is distributing flyers in my area anymore I get pretty much 100% attention when putting a flyer on a car or in someone's hand."

Let's talk about some of the tools you need for your marketing efforts. In this section we are going to concentrate on offline tools such as flyers, posters, business cards, and such.

The old school flyer had died out these past few years, but are slowly starting to make a small comeback. With social media as one of the biggest forms of new marketing, tools such as flyers and business cards were kicked to the wayside for a while. We all remember coming out of a club and having 10 flyers on your windshield. After awhile people didn't even read them and just threw them on the ground. Not very effective marketing. I don't see flyers happening much anymore in my area. See what your competition is up to.

Do I use flyers? Of course! Why? Well, since no one else is distributing flyers in my area anymore I get pretty much 100% attention when putting a flyer on a car or in someone's hand. You need to remember to keep this at a minimum and to be courteous and ethical. It is unprofessional and unethical to put flyers on cars in the parking lot of other bars. Furthermore, the city probably hates the next day clean up from people throwing them on the ground.

If I think that my target market may be receptive to flyers, I usually plan on only one week of blasting. After that, I let the social media and sub-promotion continue pressing the event, and then give a support flyer blast a few weeks in.

Now for business cards. I am talking about two different types of cards. There is the business card with your name and contact info such as "Call me to get on guest list or hire me at your club" and the promoter VIP pass that is sized exactly like a business card, but is a pass used by the customer at the door to get their VIP treatment. I love using business card-sized passes so customers can easily put them in their pocket or wallet and not throw them away. If you use sub-promoters, have a place on the card for the promoter to write in their name so that you can pay them per head accordingly. This brings you powerful word of mouth advertising with a great twist.

QUICK STORY:

I was one of the head promoters of a massive outdoor venue. Great summer spot. It had been amazing back in its day but, lost its lustre, was empty, and we needed to revive it.

We had great radio exposure, a social media campaign and flyers around the local area to get exposure rolling. It was still a slow start and needed some extra push.

So we added a Promoter VIP Card to the mix. This is how it worked: I printed 5000 business cards with the text "I'm With the Promoter - Let Me In!"

I gave these out to regulars at the venue each week so we could keep retention high. I also gave an extra stack to each of them that were interested in giving the passes out. I asked them to help out by giving them to friends that may want to check out the place.

The person with the card was able to get in past the lineup and pay only half the cover. Since our cover was $10, they paid $5. Great incentive to bring back the VIP pass and use it. I also told the person who helped me promote to write their name on the card and for everyone that came in using their VIP Pass, I offered to pay them $3.

As the place grew in numbers, my new sub promoters were making some decent money just coming out, drinking, and passing out cards to their friends. Our place was growing quickly due to this word of mouth advertising.

We still kept $2 per person at the door from customers that were a bonus to us, plus any other non-vip customers that started coming in from hearing the buzz paid the full $10 . Worked beautifully.

***

Posters are also a great way to get the word out. Use a similar design as your flyers, but make it a little more simple. People walking or driving by your poster won't have the time to read all of the text. Simplify the poster. Put pertinent information like event name, date, and venue in larger text.

Posters can be placed around town on posts, targeted retail locations (clothing, music, other spots) and even in the venue itself. Always ask permission when placing posters up in different locations. Not only do you want permission to do this so you aren't littering, but if you get their blessing it will not get cleaned up and thrown out. You may even gain some easy customers from those employees.

# TOOLS OF THE TRADE: ONLINE

## "A great way to build your email list is through your reservations and ticket sales."

Let's talk about the online marketing efforts. I'm talking about email lists, Facebook and Twitter, and websites.

As you grow your promotion business you want to capture as many emails as you can. You should have a decent list service like MailChimp, Aweber, or GetResponse that can keep your email database and easily send out email blasts.

There are a few ways to do this. One is by hiring someone to go around the venue with a clipboard or iPad on your event night and gather the information. You may want to have some type of contest, like giving away an iPad or VIP bottle service to the one lucky winner that gives you their email. This gives something back for their information and can make it easier to grab their attention.

Please make sure you do not use this information to spam people with your events. Not only will it piss them off, but they will simply remove themselves from your list and then you have lost them. You also need to be aware of any local or federal spam laws. The government is quite strict on taking email addressees and spamming people with your promotions. The fines can be hefty. So please be sure you are aware of the law and how to properly conduct your marketing.

It is fine to use the email blast with launches or ticket announcements, but don't send out the same information or event details over and over again. In your emails, use the opportunity to ask them to like your Facebook or Twitter. They may be more accepting to the advertising on their social media pages and a little more guarded when getting emails. So use emails sparingly and social media more frequently.

Another way to grab emails is directly online. Again, a great way to gain their trust and email is to have a great giveaway. Put a link to your email signup page and tell them you are gathering emails for VIP launches, private parties, exclusive early bird tickets, and more. Make sure you make it clear that you will not sell their information to anyone or spam them with constant party events. You simply want to reach out to them when you have something important to share.

A great way to build your email list is through your reservations and ticket sales. If you build an online form for collecting bottle service or guest list reservations, ask them if they would like to be automatically added to your database. Use any major event that has ticket sales to get a hold of your buyer's information and ask to add their emails to MailChimp or whichever service you are using. These are your customers and have bought tickets, booked guest list or reserved a table at your event. You are more than welcome to reach out to them to offer specials, launch announcements and more.

Your website. You should have a website that details all your events and promoted venues. Add important contact details and event details on this site. Also use the venue's website to keep their customers up to date with the events that are going on there. Insert a form on your website and the venue's website to collect guest list and bottle service reservations. Have the form instantly email you the information and keep their contact info on your database for future marketing. You can get free forms all over the internet. When our venue's start to get a ton of bookings and need better organization, we use large scale services, like Venue Driver from Las Vegas, to really organize the reservation system. We will talk more about your website further down.

Use your email database and online presence to place your event e-flyers (a web sized version of your flyer or poster). Invite all your friends and following and encourage them to share and invite as well. Let's go into social media in more depth.

# TOOLS OF THE TRADE: SOCIAL MEDIA

## "Sometimes it seems like social media changes on a weekly basis."

Facebook, Twitter, and Instagram. Let's even throw in Pinterest, Snapchat and Vine. How about any other new social media platform that is gaining ground as you are reading this?

Sometimes it seems like social media changes on a weekly basis. I'd recommend going to my blog (and there are some other amazing websites) for free posts in order to stay up to date on the ever changing social media landscape. I want to keep this book more evergreen so you don't feel that the information is dated. I have shorter ebooks offered on my website that go into more detail on topics such as Facebook advertising, viral videos, and new platforms. I keep those current as things change and offer updates to you at no charge.

Social media is definitely a key weapon in your marketing arsenal. Building up a large fan base on these sites is a great way to connect with and target your client base. Don't just post the same thing day after day. Use all the tools that social media has to offer. Post pictures, events, status updates, entertaining stories and news, and make use of Facebook's tabs for stronger interaction.

I can write an entire book on how to dominate social media. There are changing algorithms that push your posts to the top of people's news feeds, fine detailed ways to target your Facebook market when advertising, and special image sizes that look best on each different social media network. There are quite a few books and blogs out there to help you out and there is continued learning to do.

For this book I am going to assume everyone knows how to setup their own accounts and get the basic photos and upload to them. Skipping the basics, let's concentrate on how to build up your following.

A known way to build your lists are to follow others. On sites like Twitter or Instagram, search for people who have similar interests as your events as well as those who are geographically targeted. Check out competing venues and see who is following them. That is a great starter database to connect with. There isn't much use in adding people out of the country or out of your genre of events when they are never going to come and support you, so don't just click away randomly.

Have your Facebook page 'like' other pages of DJs, bands, venues, and other pertinent pages so you can clearly show that you are active in that business. Ask to join Facebook groups that fit your location and genre and be an ongoing community member in it. Add your social media links to your flyers, posters, business cards and website so you can grow your following.

Post amazing content. People like to follow your brand to get quick news on the events you are hosting, but also to be entertained. Be sure you are taking pictures at your events and post them quickly to your social media sites. Your flyers and images should be very eye catchy so it gets attention. Retweet or share great articles and pictures that your audience would enjoy. Know your market. Would a video on how to do the perfect going out makeup or a YouTube link to the newest track be entertaining to your following? Absolutely. Think of your social media account as your magazine. No one would read a magazine that is full of ads so don't make 90% of your posts about event posters and weekly event invites.

In the end, social media is just that, social. It is the online version of word-of-mouth marketing. Things can spread much quicker using social media, but you also have a lot of noise to overcome. If you can create an event or story that people get excited over, they will be your social media ambassadors that share your event to their friends and really help create viral buzz.

QUICK STORY

As a promoter, you really want to have your ear to the market and know what trends are up and coming. In my area we used to have great after hours clubs (nightclubs that are open after the regular clubs close, usually 2am - 6am). Years back they all died out. The city wanted to shut them all down and the crowd really got sketchy. People just stopped going to them and they eventually closed their doors.

For years we only had after-hours clubs in the next big city, which was an hour drive away. Well, here in my city was a market ready for the taking. After asking around to some of my sub promoters, bartenders, and regulars if they would support an after-hours scene again, I quickly found this was something they craved in the area.

So here we go. I developed a brand name, proposal to a venue owner, hammered out the revenue deal and we were on our way. I wanted to have about a month of pre-promo to get the excitement out there for launch night. So we picked a date for the launch and the promotions started.

At the beginning, I added printed flyers to the mix and distributed them around the city. However, I found that my social media marketing was the absolute biggest contributor to my promo plan. I quickly cut the offline marketing expense and pushed harder on social media.

So many people were excited about this new, local after-hours event and they were sharing my posts, retweeting my images and talking about it on their own. The biggest sign that it was going to be a great success was seeing random people creating their own Facebook event for my series each week and inviting their friends to it. Free promotion and 100% social media based.

When you create something that people care about, they will be a very large part of your social media marketing. They take it as their own and run with it.
\*\*\*

# THE RIGHT WEBSITE

## "Nothing says your club or event sucks like a shabby website from 1998."

Both your marketing company and venue(s) need to have great websites. Nothing says your club or event sucks like a shabby website from 1998.

Whether you spend big money on designers or use free tools, like Wordpress and their amazing-looking themes, please be sure you are impressive.

Most people search the web or find out about your event via social media and word of mouth. Looking at your web presence (website and social media pages) will give them an impression on what type of club you are.

Slack on your web presence and they get the impression that you also slack on the venue and fun factor. I am willing to bet that those hot clubs around your area also have great sites and, on the flip side, those venues with terrible websites have the same 'care' for their club. Where would you party if a website was your first impression on what to expect?

# GO MOBILE

## "… it is pretty safe to just assume everyone is on mobile."

Almost everyone has a smartphone nowadays. I won't quote an exact percentage because it will have increased by the time you are reading this book. With nightclub and bar clientele, it is pretty safe to just assume everyone is on mobile.

Especially in our entertainment business, pretty much everyone has a smartphone and is searching and researching on their phone. Your website needs to be mobile ready. I am not talking about your full version website fitting across the mini screen and being scrunched up into a tiny sized version. I am talking about redesigning a second mobile version of the website.

Simplifying the experience with easy tools, such as your map, click to call, guest list and reservation forms, and your upcoming event details. Those are all that is needed. You don't need to add every piece of information from your regular website on your mobile site.

Make it simple, quick and easy to navigate.

By being mobile you can also take advantage of search engine optimization on Google. Their search engine traditionally likes to line up the searcher's device with the right website. So, if a customer is looking for a local venue on their phone, those websites with a mobile version will get better rankings. Google likes to keep the user experience positive and adjusts accordingly. Take advantage of that and don't be one of the websites that are pushed down in the rankings.

How do you develop and create a mobile version of your website? There are a bunch of free services online (including Google) that can help you create a mobile version of your website. You can also outsource the work to local developers, such as your own web designer, alternatively, you can look online at services such as Fiverr or Elance and hire an outsourced developer to create one for you.

# PHONE NUMBERS AND SMS

## "They say that the open rate of SMS is over 98%"

SMS (text messaging) and phone numbers are still an important way to contact your customers. They say that the open rate of SMS is over 98%, meaning that if you send out a message it is very likely to be opened and read. Compare that to email which is around 20-30%. Even if your message gets to the recipient, they may just delete it without reading or the email could go directly into the spam folder.

Like email addresses, some people are wary of giving out their phone number. This includes their mobile phone number that offers you the ability to send out SMS messages to them. They don't want to be spammed. There is a worry that companies won't delete their info when requested and they are stuck with constant unwanted messages. So make sure they get a sense of trust from you and that their information, privacy, and time are guarded.

There are some great SMS services out there that offer inexpensive ways to utilize your list. You can have SMS contests, polls, simple announcement blasts and more. Like I mentioned previously, give them reasons to want to hear from you and make them feel special that they are part of your list.

## QUICK STORY

A nightclub I used to frequent when I was younger used the phone as their main point of contact. Way more than social media or emails. They found this had a more personal touch, in their opinion.

Everyone that called the venue to book a bottle service reservation or to be put on guest list was on their database. The club hired about 4 girls to come into the office every week and call everyone on that list.

Every Friday us 'important regulars' would get a call from one of their 'VIP Hosts' telling us how great it was to see us at the club last week on [insert date] and would like to know if we would like to be set up at our usual table. Sometimes they created a special and the call was to invite us to reserve and get some special treatment. It felt great to have that personal touch and be treated like a real VIP. Much different than receiving an email blast.

\*\*\*

# ADVERTISING

## "Up until the early 2000's ... there wasn't the same amount of marketing noise and distraction."

In your work as a promoter, marketing and advertising is key. Social media has made marketing inexpensive, but with so many events and ads being pushed within those platforms, the space has become 'noisy'.

Up until the early 2000's, a promoter could just drum up the starter funds to start a radio campaign, maybe even bring in a radio DJ or personality to host, and $2-4k per week in radio ads later, the place was jam packed. Pretty easy. There wasn't the same amount of marketing noise and distraction.

Since social media came to be, everyone can and is talking about something. Whether it is other promoters, brands and businesses, or just Joe Blow showing you what he ate today, the social media landscape is very, very crowded.

With that said, using all forms of advertising can be key in branding your event and standing out from all of the rest that use social media exclusively.

Make sure you see what your budget allows and plan accordingly. There is nothing wrong with getting some large scale buzz by using local radio. Just make sure it's worthwhile. You need a solid plan. There is nothing worse than spending $1000 over a month, getting two ads per week and not enough repetition to even be heard. On radio, get concentrated traffic of your ads. For example, if you are having a Friday event and have a small budget, pack your ads into Thursday and Friday only and not spread over two weeks. The most effective way to use radio is to have a larger budget and blast the ads every day for weeks on end, but this may not always be feasible.

Take a strong look at your local college and university media outlets. Most have their own newspaper, radio, and some even have in house ad screens around campus. If students are your target, this is definitely where you want to be targeting your advertising.

Get more from your social media by using tools like Facebook ads and boosting your posts. With the constant changes on Facebook, most of the time your post will only be seen by 5-10% of your following. So use their advertising and promoted posts tools to make sure you target thousands more potential party people.

If you are going to advertise on Facebook, be sure to target, target, target. Never setup a basic ad that targets 110,000,000 people from all over the country. Facebook has a great ad targeting system. Target by specific age, school, workplace, detailed interests such as music tastes, as well as to specific geographic location.

You can even target the ads to people who 'like' other competing bars and groups. Your ads will show up on the user's side bar or in their newsfeed and they could be a potential customer.

# GET BIG GROUPS OUT

## "When you book large parties like this you 'pad' the room with guaranteed people."

Use your social media, email database, and your website to advertise that you invite big groups to come out. Work with the venue owners to build a special promotion for birthday parties, stag and stagette parties, and office parties. Create e-flyers and get that out to your followers via email, Facebook, Twitter, and more.

When you book large parties like this you 'pad' the room with guaranteed people. Usually they come out early to get the most party time as possible, which also helps retain random customers that walk in early and see groups already out and partying.

Those groups are also mini promoters for your event as they spread the word on where they will be partying for their big night. Even a group of six people can effect decisions of others and indirectly bring 20 or more people to your place. So imagine having a few of these parties per night.

There are several different ideas that you can use for these events. Booth specials, no cover for the group, line by pass, free birthday or bachelorette party favors, a decorated table or booth, drink tickets, you get the idea.

# DEVELOP BOTTLE SERVICE AND GUEST LISTS

## "Like any business out there, a loyalty program and customer database is a major part of marketing success."

If the venue does not have a bottle service or guest list plan in action you may want to put one in place. Make sure it fits the style of the bar. Patrons of Country bars may not do bottle service at all, but perhaps still like the idea of table reservations and even pitchers or buckets of beer specials as their 'bottle'.

Like any business out there, a loyalty program and customer database is a major part of marketing success. When someone makes a bottle service booking or wants to be placed on guest list you have their contact information in hand. Treat it with respect but use it to your advantage.

You can use a few techniques to keep their information stored. If they call the venue, simply write it down on your guest list book or create a digital spread sheet. If they choose to contact and reserve online, you can create a free web form. The form should gather important information such as first and last name, email address, phone number, number of guests they are coming with, which date they wish to reserve for, and more. The form gets filled out and instantly emailed to you. Capture that information and store it for future use.

However you decide to capture the information, make sure to enter it into an organized database so that you can use it for marketing purposes.

The bottle service and guest list program gives the customer the ability to feel a bit more special than the regular customer. It gives them the satisfaction of walking past the line, having their own personal booth to sit in, the ease of pouring their own drinks from their bottle of alcohol, the private party feel at a large public venue. It retains customers and keeps repeat business coming through the door.

QUICK STORY:

At one of our venues the owner was insistent that he received all of the bottle service messages and took care of it. The club was his, so if he choose to take the messages, I wasn't going to argue. I was busy as is and it made my life easier. At least I thought so at the time.

He was a scatter brain. And to make things worse, we had 15 bottle service tables available on any given night. Since we were full on both Friday and Saturday each weekend, we would get 30 reservations during a week, plus advanced bookings for birthdays and parties booked ahead of time. You can imagine the owner's email inbox. Quite a bit of information to organize and keep track of in advance.

As you may have guessed it, some reservations were lost and forgotten and as patrons came in to the venue on their party night their booth was sold to someone else and not reserved. What a mess. As the promoter and host, I was the one that always had to deal with the irate customer.

So we implemented an online reservation system that not only took in the information using a form, but used a database and placed the right booking on the proper date. If a booth was already reserved, the customer was not able to book it and had to choose another table. So we never had double bookings. A digital version of putting a sticky note with the reservation on a calendar, but much better organized.

As a result, on any event night it was easy to log in, select the day's date, and print off the reservation list. We didn't worry about what was happening the next day or next week or next month, all of that was already organized on the system.

We just worried about the day at hand. From there on in, all reservations were digitally taken care of and customers were always happy.

*\*\**

Some added benefits to a professional system include the ability to add your sub promoters to the account and create affiliate links for them. This allows them to book reservations and build their own guest list by sharing a personal web link via their social media accounts. With that system in place you can track who they bring in and pay them accordingly. Similarly to bringing in a VIP pass with their name written on it, this was a digital solution to sub promotion.

Of course systems like these cost a bit of money per month to use, some more than others, but I have yet to find a good free system that has all of the features of a databased reservation system. It is way easier to have a system that is built for this type of service rather than taking the email yourself and using a calendar or excel spreadsheet. It starts to get too complicated as you get busy.

On some occasions the venue will pay the fee. At other times it's just worth you taking the expense and keeping yourself organized for the sake of your brand and revenue. Plus, you then have access to the database for other events.

Whether it is a free form or a professional system, put the reservation link everywhere. Put it on the venue website, your promoter website, create a Facebook tab and embed the form on those pages, share the link on Twitter and even pass that link to your sub promoters to use.

# CUSTOMER LOYALTY

"With customer loyalty, try to personalize things as much as possible."

Like any business, it is less money to keep a customer than to acquire new ones. As your business grows you will constantly be looking for new followers to come out to your party. People get bored or get older and move on. You want to keep feeding your list with fresh new people. Of course with those that do support and continue to come out to your party, you want them to come back and often. Customer loyalty is key.

Have your host (or yourself) roam around your event and meet as many people as you can. Try to remember names and treat them all like VIP's. You will quickly see how excited they are when they feel like they have a connection at the club or 'know the promoter'. Where you can, use your bar tab to buy a round of drinks.

Have a big lineup outside? Frequent your lineup and pull random groups passed the line. Use these tips on new faces as well - don't only treat the regulars like VIP and leave the new customers behind. Mix it up and build new regulars by approaching people you have never met before.

There were countless times I went out to the lineup and brought a group of people past the line. I have never met them before they were not regulars of my events at any time, but were so amazed at the treatment I gave them that they became fans for life.

If you are able to get birthday details, capture that information on your smartphone and get it into your database. Use social media to keep an eye on your Facebook pages for upcoming birthdays - the right hand bar makes it easy for you and reminds you who is celebrating. Send them a happy birthday message and invite them and their group out to your spot for a drink. Most birthday parties are large groups of friends going out to celebrate so try to get them to your event with the VIP treatment.

With customer loyalty, try to personalize things as much as possible. While an email blast to your 'loyal followers' with early bird ticket prices is a good thing to do, don't leave out the idea of personally inviting a few people with large groups. Those personalized invites work wonders and people talk and spread the word on the gracious host you are.

As word spreads that you are a great promoter, people will want to support your events. This can be especially important in this business when a venue dies out, you get replaced, or when you quit. You will eventually move to a new spot and want your following come with you.

# PROMOTER DINNER

## "Get your sub-promoters to invite all of their good looking and influential contacts for a free dinner."

What is a promoter dinner? Here is a nice way to start out your weekly event nights. Especially with venues that operate a restaurant in house as well.

Get your sub-promoters to invite all of their good looking and influential contacts for a free dinner at the venue. Make the reservation for 9:30pm so that it is early enough to not interfere with the nightlife portion of the night, but late enough to have bodies in the club at the perfect time.

Offer a dinner on the house with the caveat that everyone stays for the nightlife party. Imagine having 50 good looking people at the venue that early. By the time their dinner is completed around 11pm you already have that room padded. As other people start to arrive at the club, your place is already starting to look good - and with amazing people. If the venue has the restaurant in house the costs for a 50 person dinner is minimal to them, considering a few hundred dollars in food to kick start the night is nothing compared to thousands in advertising costs that may or may not even have a return.

You can obviously adjust this concept to fit your own venue and ideas. Perhaps if it's a venue without a restaurant, you offer a sampling party for private invite only. The venue gives a few complimentary liquor bottles for the sampling, your patron have drink tickets in hand and maybe a small catered buffet to spice up the evening. Keep an eye on your local liquor laws on free alcohol.

# PHOTOS AND VIDEO FOR PROMOTIONS

## "Be sure to get your photos and videos up as soon as possible."

A big way to get traffic to your website and social media pages is visual content. What better content to help promote your event than photos and videos of the customers? It is very important to have someone on staff to take amazing pictures and video of your event.

People love seeing themselves, they love seeing the other people that attend the event, and it's a great way for those that missed the night to capture how great it was.

Be sure to get your photos and videos up as soon as possible. Most people will message or email you asking when they will be posted if you are taking too long. I have found that after the weekend parties you want to have them up by Monday or Tuesday the latest. Everyone wants to see their party pics right away. After a few days the buzz dies down and you lose that potential traffic on your sites.

What if the night is just starting and not very busy? With that said you want your photographer to take individual pictures of the people and DJ/Band. Don't worry about a wide venue shot since it will look empty. Go around and take individual and group shots of people smiling and having fun. That hides the emptiness but also keeps the content rolling.

Be sure to add your logo, the venue logo and even quick details on the night itself. As people share photos on social media more often they probably are not going to include all of the pertinent details of the promotion, so make sure some of those details are on the pic or video. Don't make it an advertisement, but something simple like "Flirty Fridays at XYZ Club" along the bottom works well.

When talking about videos, short and sweet is usually the best tactic. This is especially true since most people will be watching the videos on their mobile phone. Less than a few minutes are great and you can make several different videos for the night. Use services like Instagram and Vine to get your videos and images to the masses.

# LET'S TALK VIRAL VIDEO

## "I wanted to see if there was a formula that could be duplicated."

I have a background in television, so I know that medium extremely well.

Recently I did a ton of research on viral videos. What makes them viral, why do they go viral, which ones are more viral than others. I wanted to see if there was a formula that could be duplicated.

Could I transfer those secrets to the nightlife biz, teach the secrets, and start to coach and produce amazing sharable content? Television production is very different than viral video development. Trust me when I say that. Two different mediums, and not just because the screen size. I am talking about the social proof aspect that changes the game entirely.

While you can't guarantee that a video will go viral, there are a few fundamental concepts that need to be used when developing and producing your video. The things that push your video into the viral scene. Without these, your video is just another TV ad and will have much less impact.

I have found that while there are a few similarities across most of the videos that have millions of views, there is also that luck factor that no one can duplicate. Right timing, right base of social followers, right topic.

Yes, you can increase your chances by advertising the video and give it a boost or plant a few influencers (people with major followers) into the mix and have them share the video for you, but again that only goes so far.

With that said, I have found that the one similarity across the board was emotion. There is always a large emotional factor in the video. Whether it is a home style video that lasts 10 seconds but is hilarious (a kid biting his brother) or a well thought out and well produced video with an amazing ending (like the recent Westjet Airline Christmas ad: http://www.youtube.com/watch?v=zIEIvi2MuEk). It is sharable. Every single viral video has the 'I need to show someone this' factor.

The majority of videos are not professionally staged videos. Many are shot on a cell phone. With all of the research I have done, people like real. They don't want to be tricked into thinking a video is real but later find everyone is an actor. They don't want to watch TV ads on the internet.

Think about the amount of times you have gone to YouTube and had to wait the 5 second countdown of an ad before you can click and skip. I am willing to bet that NO ONE sits and watches the entire ad. You count 5, 4, 3, 2, 1, Skip Ad. And why would you sit and watch it? Those videos are well produced and polished and most are actually the same TV ad that you see on TV, just put on the internet. Big deal. Not interesting. Not effective at all.

You don't need major production money to create a viral video. It does not have to be in the same quality category as a television ad. Think about different ways of featuring yourself, product, or service wrapped around an emotional strategy.

Don't always think product placement. You don't need a kid biting his brother and holding your product. Think outside of the box. Maybe the action happens at your venue. Or behind the scenes. Sometimes there is no good way to integrate your product so just leave it out, but place a 5 second slate at the end with 'Hilarious right? XYZ Venue thought so to'.

If you are going to spend the money to make the video look super professional, make sure it still falls under the 'real' category. Much like the Westjet ad that was very well produced, it was still a very real situation. None of the people were paid actors pretending their emotion. Everything was real. That is a viral video.

Think about that when creating your own video. Whether it is for YouTube, your website, Instagram, etc. What captures the viewer within 5-10 seconds? Is there enough emotion (laughing, crying, excitement, unbelievable-ism, fear, pain, etc) in it to share? Never create the same ol' TV ad for the internet. Be real. That is a key in making it social and sharable and then viral.

# CHOOSE THE RIGHT VENUE

## "Make the atmosphere work for you and choose your venue accordingly."

No matter what type of event you are producing, the venue is a very important piece of your success.

Location, location, location
While you want your party to be at the perfect location for your market you also don't want to be smothered with too many competing events. As an example, in a student market you obviously want to be close to the schools. No need to be walkable distance, but take into account cabs and how long students need to wait to get to your place. Downtown areas offer great nightlife locations but much more competition. Scout out the competing clubs. Are they killing it right now, smothering your potential location, or are they all slow and that entire area is a tough go on bringing anyone down to the area?

Ownership and Management
Promoting an event or weekly series is almost a partnership with the owner and management team of the venue. You need them to believe in your abilities, network, and concepts and give you the time and support needed to produce the people and the success.

What you don't need is ownership making decisions for you that hinder the event, or not giving you the right tools to support success such as bad staff, bad equipment, no agreed upon budget, etc. Worse yet, you definitely don't want to work with people that are going to steal from you. In this very cash-based business you don't want your cover/ticket till tampered. Work with people you like and have a mutual understanding of the success you can all enjoy.

Fitting Atmosphere
How about an electronic glow party at a country bar? Instant failure? Very, very likely. You want to choose a venue that fits the event personality. Much like the example above, you also don't want to have a country event at a dark, laser filled nightclub. Make the atmosphere work for you and choose your venue accordingly.

Using Other Nights to Support Yours
Not that this is a deal breaker, but having other full nights to help market your event definitely helps. I cannot count the number of times I went in to produce an off night (Tuesday) event that had the support of the Friday and Saturdays. Having posters and social media attention on full nights to help spread the word definitely works in your favor.

Beating a Dead Horse
On the other side of the above point, having no good nights at the venue not only gives you zero help from the venue side. This could also be a sign that it has lost its brand and allure. If it has been dead for a long while with no help from the ownership themselves, it could be possible that no event will work there anymore. Perhaps security, safety, and no longer being a hot spot could work against you no matter what you try to do there. At this point you should look right

past the venue and go elsewhere. It most likely needs to be renovated and rebranded to give new life to it.

Size Matters
Depending on the event you are producing sometimes size does matter. Capacity always comes into the fold when producing a concert. The number of tickets you can sell will dictate the ticket prices itself as well as your chances of recouping and profiting. If you are looking to do a basic residency each week size may not come into the fold as much. Just remember that a bigger venue requires more work and more people to make it look good. Smaller looks full faster, but has more limited profit potential.

Technical and Staging Requirements
Does your event require any staging and technical requirements? Instead of renting a stage, lights, sound etc. try to find a venue that has it already. No need to do a band at a small pub with no stage anywhere. On that note most agents and managers will turn down your offer if the venue just isn't going to fit their production and show concept.

In the end always trust your gut. Sometimes the old cliche is right: "If it's too good to be true, it probably is". If you have a sinking feeling that the venue, management, location, anything just isn't right - walk. Listen to your intuition. You can always find another location and make the deal and risk work for you.

# APPROACHING A VENUE

## "Depending on the type of event you wish to have, you need to look at which venues would fit best."

Now that you have decided that you want to be in the nightlife industry as a promoter, it is time to scout out a feasible venue and get a plan together for your event.

If you have absolutely no experience in promotions, you should approach a venue that you frequent with your friends and get in contact with the head promoter. Become a sub promoter there and start gaining experience and building your list, as I mentioned previously.

If you have some experience under your belt or just want to dive into your first event, then your first step is to decide what type of event you are going to promote.
Are you interested in promoting every week (a weekly event) or a one-off/special event (concert, or themed event).

Weekly events are great revenue generators for obvious reasons (you get paid every week). One-off events and concerts are also large revenue generators because you can usually charge more per person at the door with tickets, as it is not a normal weekly event.

One-offs also give you more time to promote. Usually you should plan about 6 weeks or more of promotion time for the event. On the other hand, with weekly events you are constantly working to keep the numbers growing or maintain its capacity. This is where return customers are important.

Depending on the type of event you wish to have, you need to look at which venues would fit best. You don't want to approach a pub or country bar if you are looking to do a weekly hip hop or electronic night.

Once you have your list of potential venues, take a look at those and see how they are currently doing. Do they already have hot nights that are spoken for by current promoters? What about 'too many hot nights' that can hinder your chances of being successful simply because people just won't come out to the same place multiple times a week? Is there an opportunity to create a new night and use their good branding to help push your event? Or are they empty and dying for your help, but on the flip side may not be revivable? There is a perfect balance.

Make sure you visit each venue if you haven't already. Scout them out. How is the host or door staff? Is security respectful or looking to start trouble? Are the bartenders slow and uninterested? Does the venue itself look the part? Check the place out and see what would be a concern for you.

Once you have your list of 2-3 venues it is time to approach the ownership and make a meeting.

Trying to connect with management or ownership of a venue is very hit and miss. Since they work such long and odd hours, there is no hard and fast rule on the hours they may be available to talk. Owners and managers are different in this industry. You will find that some are available during regular hours throughout the week, such as 9-5. You will find others that prefer working the nightlife hours of operation and won't be available until just before their bar opens (such as 9PM on weekends).

Make a few phone calls at different times to see if you can connect with anyone. You may get lucky and get a bartender or manager on the phone instead of voicemail. Ask when the owner is in so that you can discuss some event promotion possibilities.

Introducing yourself to the owner or manager during the busy night can work in getting a meeting as well, but remember they are busy. Keep the introduction quick and let them get back to work. Your meeting will give you time to talk in more detail.

You can also try to connect via email or social media. While it is a bit more impersonal, this avenue may be your last resort if you have a tough time getting some one on the phone or running into them in person at the venue.

When you do connect, make sure you know what you are talking about. Remember as a promoter you can be the venue's life blood. With the advent of social media, the normal avenues to marketing and promoting a venue are no long black and white. Gone are the days where a club can book a live radio DJ and a few thousand dollars of advertising gives them a guaranteed packed club. There is so much marketing noise out there, times are not easy for them. So a good promoter with ideas and a built-in list is going to catch their attention.

When you call or drop in don't just say 'I want to be a promoter for you and I can easily bring in 1000 people'.

They probably hear that 100 times a week from people. Be realistic and professional with your numbers. Tell them you would like to discuss the opportunity to run events at the venue and have a good list that can grow into a solid foundation of clients.

Get that meeting, pitch them your idea, explain how you are going to bring your list of people out and build their marketing campaign to attract even more people.

Being professional and having a professional pitch will most likely get the attention of the venue. If you are working on a pure commission basis (example, you get paid per head only) there is little risk to the ownership.

Your only concern will be having them trust that you are the right person for the job. It's great for the venue to try you out without having any risk. On the flip side, if you aren't able to move things along and pack the place, having the venue dead for another month kills their revenue and brand. For owners, time is always of the essence and every one of the venues wants their place full to capacity, now.

# NEGOTIATING THE PROMOTER VENUE DEAL

## "Having some type of paper trail of what is agreed upon is super important."

Sometimes a hearty handshake and verbal agreement is all we get these days in the nightclub and bar industry. While it makes the deal very easy to close it also opens up the door to cancel your services on the spot when the venue decides.

Can we prevent getting screwed with a written and signed agreement? Possibly. Is it worth going to court over? Sometimes.

At a bare minimum you absolutely should have your proposal written out and signed by the ownership. Having some type of paper trail of what is agreed upon is super important. Even emails or SMS messages are important to keep on file.

I cannot stress the amount of times I had major concerts on the go and had agreed on our shared responsibilities with the venue, only to have them try to back out of something like paying for flights or production. With a written agreement or paper trail on what was agreed upon I saved thousands of dollars in un-needed expenses. Shady tactics by the venue, yes. But when the show must go on it is your reputation that is on the line as well.

Please consult an attorney if you have questions or need advice on business deals and agreements. I am not a lawyer and many times verbal or written agreements were not worth pursuing when the damage was minimal. While it is the bar business at work here it has always been important to have a good paper trail on my deal. That has saved me from tricky owners who seem to 'forget' what they agreed to.

So with that said, what should you ask for in a typical promoter deal? There are so many ways to structure a deal with a venue. Here are a few typical ways that a promoter does business in this industry.

1. Promoter creates concept, pays for promoting expenses, brings in the people and keeps the cover charge as pay. Venue opens the doors, pays for staff and product and keeps all liquor sales. Sometimes the venue includes the DJ or band in their end of the staff expenses and other times it is the responsibility of the promoter. Negotiate.

2. Venue pays a flat fee for the promoter's services and pays for all expenses including the act, marketing, staff, product, and keeps all incoming revenues. Higher beginning risk on the venue but major profit potential with hard expected costs. It is similar to hiring you as their marketing guy and on a salary of sorts.

3. Promoter rents the venue, pays for all staff, security, product (liquor), entertainment, promotions, and keeps all of the cover/ticket revenue and liquor sales. Venue has zero

risk and makes a rental fee. All risk lies with the promoter but with high profit potential.

Please be sure to get all the fine details down on a proposal. Everything from who pays the cover charge girl to who holds the insurance for the venue and event.
If you are sharing risk on a concert, be sure to include who is responsible for any additional equipment (added speakers or lighting) or free liquor that the act may want in his rider. Who will pay for the rider liquor? Will the venue donate it or will they charge you for it? Do you get a complimentary bar tab to use for your guests and VIPs? When do you get paid? At the end of the night or do you take your own cover revenue home as pay?

Do you get a check every two weeks like a regular employee? Are you the head promoter, and thus you get exclusivity or first right of refusal to any new promoter trying to book an off night? Do you have say in everything that goes on at the venue from a marketing and event stand point as head promoter or just on the nights that you control?

The little things are easily forgotten but can cause a major disaster with your business relationship and event profits.

Again, an agreement is the best way to do business but many nightclub and bar owners are scared of signing agreements with promoters. They want the ability to cut the cord without any recourse. While that isn't very fair to the promoter, they have been through the murky waters of sketchy promoters with all talk and no pull. I understand their fear but build yourself a great reputation and resume of success and they will have no problem agreeing to your terms to make themselves money.

# MAKE THE VENUE MONEY

"Ultimately your venue is your client.
When they are making money you
are making money."

Ultimately your venue is your client. When they are making money you are making money. One of the hardest things to do in this business is keeping the balance of happiness between promoters and venue owners. If you are being paid a flat fee and the beginning weeks are slow you get your money, however the venue is losing money. If you take the cover charge as your pay and you bring in people but still don't break even, the venue is making liquor sales and you are in the hole.

Once you get to the point of critical mass you are in the zone. Ownership is making great sales, you are making killer money off of the door (or your fee is well justified) and everyone is happy. This is the area where you need to maintain the numbers and keep things fresh.

There is no better time for an owner to get greedy and take the reigns from you than the full house. Countless times I have had owners think they can continue my success without me and save my fee, or worse yet ask me what I am doing lately and why they still need me around (now that the event is built). Many don't realize that the marketing and maintenance is ongoing and needs constant attention. It is a very competitive market and I have seen many venues collapse after they let go their marketing and promotion groups.

Make them money and keep them in the loop with your ongoing promotions, events, ideas, hours involved, and make sure you are justifying your value and profits. A promoter can make a boat load of money every week, enough to get ownership to think twice about ongoing service with you. It could kill them, but if you can avoid it and keep everyone happy, then do it.

# LIFESPAN OF A VENUE

## "Some clubs and bars last 15+ years and others last only 6 months ..."

It can be hard to predict how long a venue can stay relevant in a market. Some clubs and bars last 15+ years and others last only 6 months before needing to renovate or rebrand.

So many factors go into the lifespan of the venue. Competition, new clubs to the area, promoters moving venues, security or safety issues, needed renovations and facelifts, management, etc.

I find that no matter how long a nightclub lasts, the promoter may have a life span of his/her own. In my experience and looking at the moving careers of fellow promoters, I have found that 2-3 years at any one venue is a good average. Many factors come into play here and, like I mentioned above, it could be local competition coming into play, stale promotions, ownership wanting to take over internally, allure of the venue is lost, etc. With that said the promoter either needs to move on or is forced out so that the owners can try something new.

The same goes for the entertainment. I find that DJs, bands, and hosts. follow in the same lifespan. Owners and managers see the success start to dip at a certain point and need to try something new to change things up.

If continue your business with a high profile, treat your promoting company seriously and keep things very fresh, you can expand your own lifespan per venue. Just stay very relevant, listen to the customers, and keep a good eye on the trends.

Whether you expand the span of your promotions at any particular venue or move on to the next, you can have this entertainment business grow and succeed for many, many years.

# ONE-OFF EVENTS OR THEME PARTIES

"There are so many ideas you can come up with for a one-off event and you can keep costs relatively low."

From weekly residency nights to concerts you will find some fantastic revenue developing one-off events. These themed nights can range from a Glow Party to Halloween to New Years Eve to Mardi Gras.

Creating the right theme, decor, staff costuming, and marketing materials all come into play here. Like any other promotions you need to get the word out using social media, flyers, posters in the venue and surrounding areas, and use your sub promoters to promote with you.

Some quick ideas:
Glow Party (glow sticks and UV lights)
Country Party
Mardi Gras
Easter Bunny Night
Halloween
Devil's Night
Naughty Santa Christmas

Homecoming
All White Party (everyone wears white)
All Black Party (everyone wears black)
Liquor or Beer branded night (ie Smirnoff party)
Superbowl Party
Toga Party
ABC (wear Anything But Clothes - people really get creative!)

There are so many ideas you can come up with for a one-off event and you can keep costs relatively low with decor, costuming, and a resident DJ or band. Kick it up a notch by booking a larger DJ or band to play at the event and make it a small concert wrapped into the themed night.

# OTHER PARTY CONCEPTS

## "There are a few other tried and true event ideas that work when done right."

There are a few other tried and true event ideas that work when done right. Let's talk about a few here.

Pre and Post Parties
These are themed around a specific event. Examples can include a Post Concert Party. Most large scale arena concerts end around 11pm so the ability to continue to party locally is a great way to get customers through the door. If you have the budget, try to get one of the band members or DJ's to make an appearance at your after party. If not, you can always make it an unofficial post party. Alternatively you can use your connections with an act's management and get the right permissions to make it an official after party.

Keep an eye on local convention centre events, sporting events, TV shows, and more. See what is going on during certain dates in your area and create a great themed party to go with it.

After Hours
Some people just don't want to go home. When the bar or club closes there are always groups of people looking to continue their partying. Some will end up at late night restaurants and others will crave the continuation of

nightlife. Most after hours parties that are public have been in the electronic music scene.

Without alcohol being served at an after hours party and the limited available parties, you usually charge a premium at the door. The venue may want a piece of that cover charge money since they are losing liquor sales, but they should also be aware that they can charge a premium for items such as energy drinks, water bottles, and even food.

With so many bars and clubs in any market and probably only one after hours club (yours!) you can target every single patron of those regular venues as potential customers. Now don't get me wrong, just because there are thousands of people leaving bars and clubs on a specific night that does not mean that they are all looking for an after hours event. They may be tired, drunk or just not interested in that scene. Your market share will be targeted, but with that said you should get the promotions out there just like any other event and continue your revenue streams to the early hours.

Pub Crawls
These are fantastic during special occasion weeks such as Halloween, Frosh Week, Easter, St. Patrick's Day, and Christmas. I know some promoters that only run a few bar crawls every year as their only source of income. They connect with local venues and promoters and sell Pub Crawl wristbands to thousands of people.

They pick several official bars to visit during the night and the wristband offers free entry. Most of the time the venue offers a drink special as part of the pub crawl. The venue wins because they get large groups of people on off nights or earlier than usual on regular nights where they would normally have zero sales. The promoter wins by organizing the event and making money off each wristband sold.

# ALL-AGES EVENTS

## "… sometimes it is smart to develop all-ages events as a farm team for the club."

I have heard the concerns time and time again. "All ages events are a pain in the ass". The majority of the time these complaints come from either the security who think there is nothing but problems with these 'kids', from the bartenders who know they won't be selling alcohol so don't make good tip money, or from the owners who complain about the amount of revenue they lose due to the inability to serve alcohol.

I tell every one of those people that sometimes it is smart to suck it up and see all-ages events as a farm team for their club. If you really look at the possible benefits to having an all-ages event, you can quickly look past any of these perceived issues and leverage the opportunity to promote and prime these kids up for your venue. As they get older and can legally get in to your regular nights, where do you think they are going to party? Think farm team.

If there are very few all-ages parties going on in your area (or none at all), this allows you to charge a premium cover at the door. As the promoter, be sure to offer a healthy split with the venue owner to compensate for their lost revenue on liquor. The security should be fairly happy to get another work night and more hours on their time sheet and, to be honest, all ages events don't cause any more issues or fights than any other regular bar night. As for the bartenders, selling water, energy drinks, and sports drinks are still beverage sales and offer similar chances to make tips. Maybe the owner can offer to pay a little more hourly salary on those nights to compensate.

Your biggest mission is targeting these young customers. You cannot go onto high school property with flyers and hand them out. You also shouldn't add them to your Facebook and Twitter account and mix your under age and of-age list.

Your best mode of advertising is going to be traditional advertising. Here you may need to spend some money on radio ads and social media ads that are highly targeted to their age group and interests.

A big way to promote is with a young street team of sub promoters that can spread the word out to their school friends and invite their own social media friends to your event. You may have younger siblings or cousins you can access. There might be someone who works at the venue who may have access to the younger crowd, which you could utilize. Hire a young local DJ or two for opening sets and have them get the word out. Get these people on board as a promoters and offer them a per head commission for tickets they sell.

Create a separate all-ages Facebook and Twitter account and start making a second database for this age group. Use the methods mentioned in this book to capture that information when they are at the event and now you have a new list to use when producing these all-ages parties. As they grow older, move their info to the regular list to keep things fresh.

With nothing for that age group to do besides house parties, you can really get a hold of that market and the event will be a huge success.

# HOW I TURNED $50 INTO $1000

## "… everything in life can be negotiated and many venues, as well as promoters, are looking for more ways to make money."

Here is a fun story. I was head promoter for a large size club and our Friday and Saturday were bringing in 1000 people each night, on average. Great student clientele.

Another promoter team approached me to throw a Glow Party. For those not familiar with these kinds of parties, they are electronic DJ 'rave' type parties with a ton of glowsticks and black lights. Most people come dressed to theme with neon colors and glow away! A great party concept and our market loved that type of thing.

We already knew we had the audience in our hands. With my Friday and Saturday parties going, so this wasn't going to cost us too much in advertising as I was able to put up posters in the club. I wouldn't be trampling on someone else's traffic since it was my own network and clientele.

I had full control of the venue's Facebook and Twitter accounts as well as being their head promoter, so that was going to be another advantage marketing wise. On top of all of that, I had my own promoter company's Facebook and

Twitter network and the other promoter had his. We had a fantastic marketing network when put together.

Since we were already full on the weekend, we decided to throw this party on an off night, a Tuesday. The club was always closed on that day so everyone was going to win here.

The other promoter had great internal designers who made up the poster and web flyer at no added cost to us. I had 20 posters printed at our Staples/Kinkos for $20. I placed them all over the club two months in advance so that people would be aware of the event. We used the web version of the flyer to create Facebook events and blasted that out to all of our social media outlets, again with zero cost. We went to our local dollar store to buy glow bracelets. They had 20 for $1 so we bought 600 glow bracelets to give out for free on the night of. This cost us $30.

On the night of the event, one of us was at the door taking cover charge, therefore not requiring to hire someone to cover the door. Our DJ friend offered to do the night for a $50 guarantee, but if it was profitable, bonus up to $200. We invested $50 initially and brought in 450 people at $5 each. Do the math: 450 x $5 equals $2250, minus the DJ ($200) and our expenses ($50) leaves $2000 for us to split down the middle.

I know what you may be thinking, this is easy for me to say since I had control over many aspects of the promotion and venue while most outside promoters wouldn't get that luxury. True. But everything in life can be negotiated and many venues, as well as promoters, are looking for more ways to make money.

Think about it from the other promoter's end. He didn't have the same luxuries I had and had no 'in' to my club, but when he approached me to work together on an outside idea, I was definitely interested. By teaming up with me, those other promoters partnered in and therefore took advantage of the same luxuries I had.

Promoters can't do it all and shouldn't be greedy. Sometimes it's nice to work with someone else and take some pressure off the work load and promotions.

With that said, if you have a killer idea for a promoter or exclusive access to something that a promoter or venue wouldn't have (do you have your own DJs, foam machine, a large list, or just a willing to work hard?) Use it! Approach the head promoter of a venue and talk about doing an off night. Give the promoter a great incentive to help you get it off the ground and close the deal.

I have since worked with these promoters on several events and made some consistent money.

# LET'S TALK CONCERTS

## "With big money to be made there is also large risk involved and that could lead to major losses."

Here is a major part of a promoter's business. If you have built a large following, have been in the business awhile, and are adventurous enough, you may want to get into concert booking and promotions.

The concerts I am talking about are nightclub concerts, not necessarily massive arena concerts. These can be bands or DJs that can fill a venue with 500 - 1000 capacity. Their fees can range from a few hundred dollars to several tens of thousands of dollars. So you really need to know your numbers and what the market can handle.

With big money to be made there is also large risk involved and that could lead to major losses. You need to be ready for this and be able to roll with the punches and continue business if you take a loss.

Off Nights
There is nothing wrong with choosing an off night to produce a concert. An off-night is usually a weekday such as a Monday or Tuesday. Most venues are busy during the weekend and have the weekdays wide open to offer their place for a show. If you look at the concert schedules in large arenas you will quickly see that many of them are presented

on off nights. You can follow the same path and get a great rental deal from the venue and sometimes a reduced fee from the artist as well.

Production and Hospitality Costs
Keep in mind that most of the time the promoter is responsible for the travel, accommodations, and the added production of the concert. Even though a venue may have their in-house sound and lights, a band or DJ may want their show to look extra special and request added equipment and lights to be put in. Those expenses are yours to take care of unless you can negotiate those costs to be looked after by the venue.

Flights or ground travel may be added to your expenses when booking an act. Be sure to ask the agent what costs are not included in their fee. Find out how many hotel rooms the act needs. They usually need more than one to accommodate their manager or crew. Negotiation is key; you can sometimes include these things into the fee as a buyout, but the industry standard is that these are an extra cost to you. Just be aware of the add-ons and don't get a surprise.

Promoters Are Key
There are many agents, managers, and artists that like to follow the promoter more than the venue itself. Don't be discouraged if your venue of choice has not booked acts in the past. If you build a good reputation with these managers and acts, they will know that you put on a good show, you choose venues wisely, and you take good care of their clients. Since you are the buyer and promoter, they feel comfortable with you and may look past a venue without a reputation. That being said, there are circumstances where the venue just isn't what fits their brand and the artist doesn't want to play there.

Start by booking smaller acts as it is easier for the agents to accept your offer and build trust and a name for yourself. Then you can move into the major artists and the big money.

Punch the Numbers
No matter how good a deal sounds I always punch the numbers. I have an excel sheet that I created which lists all the expenses that could come into play when producing a concert. That sheet also allows me to insert my ticket pricing, venue capacity and shows me the break even numbers.

It sounds great when so-and-so is available for XX amount of dollars, much lower than their usual fee, but after punching the numbers the market still cannot accept the required ticket pricing and you can't make money. Don't fall into the hype of the act and the fee they are offering. Sometimes it just doesn't work out. Make sure you always look at the expenses and amount of tickets you can sell first.

How to Set the Right Ticket Price
Ticket pricing is very important. It could make or break your concert and profit margins. Tickets that are priced too high cause the market to stay away and no one will buy. Tickets too low and you may have a sell-out, but minimal profits or even worse still a loss.

Take a look at the other venues in your city and their ticket prices for concerts. Then look at the artist and what type of prices they can command in other cities. Be aware that the agent will try to charge the standard going rate for an act whether your market is Las Vegas, Minnesota, Toronto or Niagara Falls. However since the ticket prices they can command in each market will differ, use the marketing knowledge wisely to negotiate the best possible artist fee.

This is where knowing your market comes into play. Can a band that gets $50 tickets in Vegas get $30 in Fort Lauderdale? With that number how many tickets can you sell at the venue? Work those numbers and see if the agent's offer can be profitable. Most agents want the most money for their client so you need to make sure they understand your market and venue capacity so that the fee can benefit everyone involved.

Selling your Tickets

A great way to launch a concert is to have early bird tickets and scale the pricing up as time moves on or as tickets are sold. Don't sell too many at the lower early bird prices. While you want to have immediate sales and buzz, you also want to make sure you make a decent profit for your work. Plan to have a good balance set.

Once your early birds are gone be sure to promote that they are sold out and advanced tickets are next. Many promoters use the following scales: Early Bird, Advanced, General and at the Door Price. Again, punch your numbers so that all ticket pricing is accounted for and your profit margins work out.

Local Acts

A great way to gain buzz and ticket sales is to have a local act open for the headliner. You can create a contest for local acts to promote their music and have people vote on their favorite opener. This creates fantastic early buzz for your show at the same time. The local act that has a great following will help in ticket sales when their fans come to see them open for a big concert. Also, they may wish to help sell tickets on their own and get the standard cut of the commissions. That helps them make money over and above their small opening fee. Keep an eye on those great local acts and file them away for future concerts.

Proper Promotion Time
There is no hard and fast rule on the amount of time you need for promotion. Our team likes to have about 45-60 days of sales time to get the word out properly. I have done as little as two weeks and as long as 4 months of promo time. It really depends on what your actual promo schedule looks like, what other concerts have been booked around your area or at the venue, and how hard you need to work to get the word out.

The Venue Promoter Split
In some cases there will be a split between you and the venue. Most deals are simplified like so: Venue opens the doors and offers the club at no fee or discounted rental, pays for the security, staff, venue, etc. and keeps the liquor sales as profit; Promoter pays for the artist, promotions, rider and keeps the ticket sales as profit.

The above is a standard deal, but can be lopsided at times. Usually the venue has the same hard costs to be open at any day of the month, so one added off-night is no difference (ie rent, heat, electricity, etc) and the added staff costs are very minimal (a few hundred dollars most of the time for the extra staff). So their profitability ratio is much better. On the other hand, the promoter must factor in the fee for the DJ or band, promoter commissions, flyers and tickets, hotels and travel for the act, etc. Ticket prices have to be calculated properly in order to hit profits.

With that said, there have been times where the promoter and venue are able to negotiate a better evenly shared deal. Sometimes the venue pays for some of the artist, other times they split door and liquor down the middle (with all expenses also equally split).

Gone are the days where the venue has the upper hand and should be commanding minimum bar sales, large rents or deposits. With the market the way it is there are more empty venues than good promoters. Use that to your advantage to negotiate a fair deal so that everyone wins.

## QUICK STORY

There are a few times where the standard deal just did not work out. Imagine a DJ that costs upwards of $20,000 and a standard promoter venue deal that gives the venue all the liquor sales with their regular staff expenses and the promoter all of the ticket revenue with the artist expenses.

On this particular evening, there was a snow storm. While it is out of everyone's hands the show still did well at 600 people. With that said, however, the venue made a killing at the bar with over $12,000 in sales while the break even number for the show was at 550 people, giving the promoters pretty much no profit at all.

Yes there is a risk involved in concert promotion, but the standard deals can really make a great party seem like a hassle if there is no profit in it.

You see, the venue's break even number was probably 100 people, with their security and staff costs being much lower than the DJ and concert expense. A little lopsided. Be aware of your numbers and try to negotiate accordingly.

***

# NEGOTIATING THE TALENT CONTRACT

## "Don't get discouraged if you get ignored after umpteen emails to different agents."

There are a few steps in securing and negotiating talent for your live event/concert. One of the hardest things to do is reach out to the agency and get a response. You have to imagine these agencies are getting inquiries about famous acts all day long and trying to filter out who is serious and who is just 'kicking the tires'.

The more you book the better your reputation in the industry will be and agents will be open to respond to your inquiries. Don't get discouraged if you get ignored after umpteen emails to different agents. A great way to get your foot in the door is to work with an established promoter to book your acts. This puts the promotion of the concert under your resume and helps give you credibility when you are emailing or calling agencies on your own behalf.

I have found that acts and management loves to work with promoters they know, have worked with before, and are comfortable with. They want to know they will be properly taken care of. Ground transportation is waiting for them at the airport, hotel is of proper standard, the venue is safe and ready to go technically, and the promotions have been in place so they have a full show. As you build that reputation you will start to get constant emails from agencies offering upcoming and established acts for you to book.

The reputation also helps you negotiate better deals with the act. Saving thousands of dollars on talent fees helps your bottom line tremendously. Lower your risk and increase your profit potential.

There are two basic ways to pay the talent; the flat guarantee and the back end deal. The flat deal is basically the straight up fee they are asking for. If they want a $10,000 flat fee, that is the fee. If you are able to negotiate a back end deal, then the guarantee is lower and the act takes part in the profits. I have seen less and less of this deal (the acts don't care to take part in the risk or try chasing sales and accounting of the promoter to be sure they are not missing any money), but if you can swing this deal it definitely helps.

With a backend deal example an act may instead agree to a $4000 guarantee instead of $10,000 however also take 80% of the ticket profits (ie after all agreed expenses are paid the act gets 80% you take 20%). The profits are much lower, but the initial risk of the act is also much lower in the event that you flop and lose money. With this type of deal the agent will ask you for a spread sheet of all expenses that you will encounter.

Once agreed upon, that number is all that you are able to claim off the ticket sales as expenses. The rest is profit to split. Be sure you don't forget to include anything or have last minute disasters creep up on you.

Here is a tip, why not include your promoter fee in the expenses and then the 20% profits become your investor revenue. See what you can negotiate.

What are the steps in booking talent?
First you need to send an inquiry email or phone call to the agent. Usually the act's website or social media page has the booking information (agent name and email). Send them an inquiry email with lots of details. Know your event and make them know that you are already well versed in your market, date, and venue details.

Add a quick opening paragraph introducing yourself, your background, and past acts and concerts you have produced. Then add the act that you are interested in, the concert date, venue name and city. Include the capacity of the venue and the ticket levels you are going to sell (example: early bird $20 x100 tickets, advanced $30 x200, general admission/door price $40 x400). This is obviously a guesstimate, but it does give the agent some numbers to work with. They will then come back with the act's regular fee and you can determine if it will fit within your budget and sales potential.

When they reply with the artist's availability and fee, you can start the negotiations with an offer sheet. Usually the agency has their own word document that needs to be filled out. The Offer Sheet and has all sorts of questions and details. Much like your initial email, you need to fill out venue details, sales details, etc. They will also want to know what marketing you may have in place (radio, social media, etc), local hotels that they can choose from (pick three that are of high quality and close to the venue), and also what airport(s) are close to the venue. The Offer Sheet is also where you put your event date and official fee offer to the artist. Usually you want to be close to the fee that the agent quoted you, but I do like to see what I can push. If I can save a little bit on the fee and use that money towards marketing, I definitely will try.

Next is the waiting game. The agent will present your offer to management and they will look it over. Accepting your offer sometimes takes a bit of time. Several factors can come into play here. Is the fee what they are looking for? Is it an off night or off tour and they are looking to make some added money? Is a potential tour coming around and your event will be right in the middle of it, making their travel a nightmare? Is there a competing venue with an offer on the table as well? What about a venue that is in an outside city but wants a large radius clause (a clause that stipulates that no one can book the act in the city and surrounding areas, giving their event the largest possible pool of ticket buyers)? So many factors come into play here as management considers your offer.

If your offer is accepted, consider it a binding agreement at this stage. While there are occasions where you can back out, since you have not signed the final agreement and some fine details may allow you to back away, it is definitely frowned upon and now in their calendar and booked. The official contract will come your way with fine details on how to pay and all of the technical and rider requirements. Read these over and make sure nothing out of the ordinary is in there. Typically you will see flights from their home city to yours as an expense, ground travel from the airport to the hotel and venue (and then back to the airport the next day), hotels for the night, any added technical requirements for the stage, and a meals plus liquor rider for their green room.

After the agreement is signed (they will also sign and send you a fax or copy) you can send in your deposit. Most likely a first time booking will require you to send in 100% of the fee so that they know you will not back out of the event, or their remaining balance. However it is standard to only pay 50% of the fee and the balance the night of (before the act starts). So it never hurts to ask for this even as a first time booker.

This is great since you can leverage only half of the required bulk investment and start selling tickets for the show, creating your revenue and cash flow for the rest of the expenses.

After signing and sending in the deposit have your designer create your posters. You need to send in your marketing materials to the agency (posters, flyers, etc.) for approval and once approved you will be given the green light to announce the show and start selling tickets!

QUICK STORY:

I had sent an offer in for a hip hop act. We negotiated a doable fee and very nice radius clause. The act has never been to the market and was hot on the radio. Everything looked like the show was going to be a great success. With the radius clause in the offer no other surrounding city was able to jump on our event and do a second night. We were the only ones in the area and that increased the chances of out-of-towners buying tickets and travelling in.

I received the agreement and everything looked fantastic and what we agreed on. Then I looked at the hospitality rider (where the flights and hotel requests were); it asked for 14 flights and 14 suites for the act, his management, and entourage. I quickly called the agency and said this was out of the ordinary to pay for all of his friends to come out. I didn't mind the typical act, manager, security flights and hotels, but if his entourage wants to come and party it was not going to be on my dime. The agency said it is out of the norm but standard on this particular acts rider. Signing the agreement also meant I agreed to all of the rider particulars, and of course after asking management to adjust the ridiculous request without success I told them they were hindering the ability for me to profit from the show and did not accept the agreement.

We mutually agreed to back out of the offer without harm (nothing is ever announced until the contract is signed, deposit is sent, and marketing materials approved) and thank goodness I read over every page of each document they sent.

***

# GET YOUR TALENT ON VIDEO

## "Be a professional host and don't ask silly or risqué questions. Make it fun."

If you are able to get approval from management you should always try to get your big act to send you a video promo. They can use their mobile phone and shoot a quick video since you don't need studio quality video.

The idea is to have them help in the promotion of your ticket sales. "Hello this is DJ XYZ and I am coming up to CITY to party with all of you! I heard your city is by far the loudest crowd in the country, I can't wait to experience it!!" Post that video everywhere. Most acts share their own tweets or Facebook posts as the event gets closer but this promo video will help early on.

When the act is at the venue another great tool is a quick video interview. This needs to be approved by their management but if you happen to get a quick 2-5 minute interview on camera you can use that for your event company, venue exposure, next concert, and more. Be a professional host and don't ask silly or risqué questions. Make it fun.

While it is great to have footage of the actual concert itself please remember that you cannot record the entire concert (as a live shoot) and use it. That is against copyright laws.

Whether it is on video or you record the set on audio, without permission to do this you can get in hot water.

# TICKET SALES

## "One of the greatest ways to sell your tickets will be online."

Selling tickets to your events or concerts is usually your only source of revenue. Sponsorships are not usually easy to obtain, even from liquor brands, so you need to be sure you have a great system in place to get the most sales possible.

Online Tickets
One of the greatest ways to sell your tickets will be online. You have full control of the sales and tracking and the money goes directly into your own bank account. There are many services out there so make sure you have a good look at which fit best. Services such as Ticketmaster, Eventbrite, Venuedriver and more all have amazing systems to accommodate your needs. A quick Google search will bring up many more so have a look and see which one fits your needs.

Make life easy on yourself and use only one. Not only is it confusing for your customers to see your event posted on several different ticket selling sites, but it will be even more of a pain logistically come event time when you have several styles of tickets coming to the door. All are legit, but imagine the pain of telling the gate staff that two different styles are emails from two companies, one style is a printed ticket from promoters, another is just an online print out, etc. What a mess. Simplify where you can.

## Hard Tickets

The second avenue in ticket sales is the hard ticket (the actual printed ticket). Again a quick Google search and you will find countless printing companies that will accommodate your needs and send you top quality counterfeit-proof tickets. I always print enough for the capacity of the club and destroy tickets as the online ones get sold. This way you can't over-sell the show. Imagine the PR mess if someone shows up with a ticket and the venue is at capacity. If you sell 10 online tickets go rip up 10 hard tickets. Numbers stay accounted for this way. Get these tickets to retailers, opening acts, sub promoters and the venue itself. Create a deal to pay a cut of the ticket price as a commission on sales so people are motivated to help you sell the show.

## Retail Locations

There are always a few great retail locations that are willing to be a part of a great event. You can add their logo to the flyers or tickets and also give them a commission on the sales too. Make sure you have an agreement written out which outlines their responsibility to sell and collect money on your behalf and pay you the ticket amount minus their commission. Give them low amounts of tickets to start and write down the ticket numbers they are given. Have them initial this agreement as well. Check on them frequently to see how many they have sold, collect the cash in hand, and see if they need anything to support their sales like posters, flyers, more tickets, etc.

Once you have a few retail locations in your market that sell well and you trust, you will have built a very nice brick and mortar sales network.

Ticket Sellers and Sub Promoters
These promoters hit the streets, tell their friends, use social media, and more. Like the retail locations make sure they are accountable for their tickets. Have them sign an agreement with their ticket numbers printed off so everyone knows what they have in hand. Check on them frequently to get a sold count, collect the cash coming in, and top them up with new tickets.

QUICK STORY

You really need to be on top of your ticket sellers and retail locations. My advice is to give them small amounts (20 tickets) to start with and as they bring in your cash from sold tickets you can give them more.

On a few occasions, this one particular venue gave a ticket seller over 100 tickets to go sell and did not manage their sellers well (ie had no agreement or ticket numbers written down).

When the time came for the sellers to come in with the cash, this one seller had only sold 10 tickets. This held up inventory in his pocket instead of out on the street with another seller that was able to move them, but even worse he claimed that he only received 50 in total. So there were 50 tickets missing from this person.

Did he sell them and keep the cash in his pocket? Did he lose them and then claim he only had 50 so that he wouldn't have to pay for the tickets out of his own pocket? The venue manager was angry but had no agreement or real proof on which tickets this seller had in hand.

On another occasion a ticket seller had 20 tickets in hand, sold them all, but had no cash when it was time to collect. He had sold them to friends that were going to 'pay him later'. With a proper agreement the seller was responsible for the ticket cash come event day and had to pay in full for the 20 tickets and go collect from his friends to recoup his costly mistake.

So please be very careful when it comes to ticket sellers and build a trustworthy network of sellers.

***

# SPONSORSHIP

## "Think outside of the box when presenting your idea to sponsors."

While it is hard to get sponsor money to help you throw events for small and medium sized events, it is possible to get sponsors on board for in-kind services.

Marketing Support. Retail stores, radio stations, and newspapers may want to help you sponsor your event to give their brands some added awareness in return for promotional help. They may trade ad space or poster space in their stores. You add their logo and branding on your marketing materials and it is a win-win situation.

Liquor Companies may want to get involved somehow with donating branded swag, prizing, and sometimes even complimentary liquor (sampling) for your event. Again this helps spread their brand awareness to your network and in turn you get a hold of some great items to give away at the event.

Money Sponsors. When you produce a large scale event like a concert you have a better chance at attracting a money sponsor. Usually the sponsor will give cash in return for being the presenting partner. They are put on all marketing materials, ads, and tickets, and know that with a large event they will get decent exposure for their investment. With smaller club events, weekly residencies, etc. these money sponsors usually don't get enough exposure to make it worth their investment.

Think outside of the box when presenting your idea to sponsors. Use everything from posters, flyers, social media, tickets, banner placement, website, mobile app, putting a car out front with their logo, anything that can expose their brand in a catchy way. There is so much noise out there in the world and everyone's message can get lost. A company's marketing objective is to get eyeballs on their brand and message. Help them get those eyeballs with an exciting concept.

QUICK STORY

A friend of mine owns a hair salon. With experience in promoting, he keeps his salon at the forefront of 'cool' and exciting by producing concerts a few times a year. His salon is the presenting sponsor.

The salon logo is all over the concert marketing, tickets are sold at the salon itself, and the residual social media effect by adding concert pics, celebrity video of their hair and makeup done at his salon are well worth the promotional investment.

***

# BE DILIGENT WITH YOUR CALENDAR

## "Always know what is going on around you so you can plan properly and not get caught."

This is pretty important for any event planner. When you are getting into the promotions game, you need to know what is going on around you and when people are away or ready to party.

As an example, if your target market is students you better know their exam and holiday schedule. When are their final papers due? Midterms? Major tests? Final exams? You can imagine that during these weeks the students are going to be bogged down in their school work. Don't discount the week leading up to those times as well. For a final paper due, the weeks before will be work time for them so your venues may be slower. Also keep an eye on Spring Break weeks. These dates may differ between college and university even in the same city.

Get on the school's website and look for their calendar of events. You can find some great information there. Mark them down on your own calendar.

Next, be sure you mark down all the major holidays so you can prepare and plan ahead for big themed parties. St. Patricks Day, Valentines, Halloween, New Years Eve, Easter Weekend, and more. Sometimes these holidays have a great 'day off' placed in the perfect spot. For example, the Easter holiday gives you Good Friday. Traditionally this is a day off for many people, so plan an amazing Thursday event!

Another reason to keep an eye on these dates is to prepare for slower times at the venue, since people aren't going to come out. Most places slow down over Christmas and Christmas Eve. People are with family and many don't stray away. Some do still go out, but know your market and what to expect in terms of your number.

Finally, always keep an eye on your competition. While everyone is going to have a Halloween event, you need to make sure you keep an eye on competitive one-off events or concerts so that you can climb over the market competition.

I can't stress enough the importance of this. I have seen it over and over again: a promoter books a major concert and pays $20,000 for a DJ that would otherwise be a great success, only to find that another, even bigger DJ has been booked the night before in the same market. This kills their ticket sales and they lose huge amounts of money.

Always know what is going on around you so you can plan properly and not get caught. This is another reason why I like to be friends with other promoters. We keep each other informed as much as possible, keeping our competitive edge where necessary but also make sure we don't jump over the same acts or dates.

# OPENING NIGHT OF YOUR EVENT

"Sometimes events take weeks to build up and have the buzz spread."

When doing a weekly series that first night can be a scary one. Even when you have amazing promotions and buzz all over the city you still have no idea what to expect. Will it be packed? Will it be a slow start? How long does it take for people to want to check it out? So many unknowns and, yes, sometimes opening nights are not instant successes. Sometimes events take weeks to build up and have the buzz spread.

How can we help the night out? Do a launch special. Special invites for your regular network, venue VIPs, friends and family. Have them come to the venue an hour early and offer them drink specials or free food. That gives your event a nice starter room pad of people as the night kicks in and your regular marketing comes to life.

# CONCLUSION

## "Always be learning."

The nightlife industry is one of the most fun businesses you can get into. If you are super social and can handle the music, late nights and partying, this can be very successful for you.

Build your network of friends, put them on a list (SMS, email, social media, anything) so you can reach out and connect with them. Stand out from the noise of social media and advertising by thinking way outside the box, both with your events and your marketing tactics.

Always be learning. I read books on a constant basis. Everything from *The 4 Hour Work Week* to the *Viral Video Manifesto* to *Billboard Magazine* to Industry and Social Media Blogs. You must always have your eye on business and marketing trends and have your ear to the ground for music and entertainment trends. You need to be the creative force behind developing event concepts and marketing them.

If you ever have questions please reach out to me. I love sharing my experiences and creativity.

Thank you for taking the time to read and learn from my experiences.

Enjoy the lifestyle!
Louie La Vella
louielavella.com | @louielavella

# APPENDIX A: SAMPLES

Here are some very usable sample agreements, materials and forms.

1. Sample Promoter Venue Agreement
2. Sample Talent Agreement
3. Sample Offer Sheet (to talent's agency)
4. Sample Weekly Night Expenses

## — — —Sample Promoter Venue Agreement— — —

Promoter/Venue Hire Agreement

This agreement is made between Night Club Ltd. Holyrood Court, London SE1 2EL ("The Venue") and X ("The Promoter") Address; X

This agreement applies to the hire of the venue on:
• X – 22:00pm – 06:00am on DATE

1. Promoter's Rights & Obligations
(i) The Promoter shall not be entitled to admit people exceeding the agreed capacity, including but not limited to all paying, guest list and VIP guests and the Promoter's artists and staff.
(ii) The Promoter shall be responsible for ticketing the event in accordance with the venues minimum age and entrance policies.
(iii) The Promoter shall be responsible for the promotion of the event.
(iv) The Promoter shall be responsible for the booking and payment of all DJs and performing artists appearing at the event.
(v) The Promoter's tickets, promotional materials, and use of the club logo must be approved by the Venue prior to public use.
(vi) The Promoter shall have access to the Venue for set-up no earlier than 2 hours before doors on the day of the event, unless otherwise agreed by the Venue.
(vii) The Promoter must strike and remove all production materials, stands and other items brought in for the event, immediately after the event.

(viii) The Promoter shall be responsible for the cost of additional sound & lighting equipment, which falls outside of the Venue's provided specification.

(ix) The Promoter shall be responsible for the cost of any additional sound engineers or lighting engineers required / requested as a result of the Promoter's additional production set-up.

(x) The Promoter must take all reasonable steps to ensure that illegal fly posting or flyering does not occur under any circumstance.

(xi) The Promoter must always act in the best interests of The Venue and do as much as is reasonably practicable to protect The Venues licence.

(xii) The Promoter will provide the venue with a guest list allowance of at least 20 names for each event.

(xiii) The Promoter shall be liable for the costs of any damage caused to the venue during set-up and strike of their production.

(xiv) The Promoter can choose to allocate a number of tickets for venue to sell. Details of this to be agreed as per each gig.

2. Provision of Venue

(i) The fee for the hire of the venue under the terms of this agreement is X. The Venue will provide The Hirer with the use of the following rooms: Main Room. Additional rooms may occur additional costs and should be written into this agreement.

(ii) It is venue policy that the Promoter must use two of the Venue's Front of House staff to manage tickets and guestlist unless otherwise agreed. Front of House staff are charged at £X per hour per person with a minimum payment of £X each.

(iii) The Promoter shall be responsible for the running of their till.

(iv) The facilities provided by the Venue to the Promoter shall include:
- Security Team
- Sound / Lighting
- Management Staff
- Fully Stocked Bar, Bar Staff
- Cloakroom & Cloakroom Staff
- Toilet Attendants
- Venue Clean
- Additional staff can be hired by the venue but this will be an additional cost for the hirer
- Any additional costs outside of the venues usual setup must be paid for by the promoter e.g. VIP security staff, additional DJ equipment

3. Venue's Rights and Obligations

(i) The Company's liability in contract / Venue Hire Agreement, tort or otherwise (including but not limited to any liability for negligence) however arising out of or in connection with the performance of its obligations under this Agreement for all events or series of connected events occurring for the hired event of this Agreement, shall not exceed in the aggregate 100% of the Hire Fees / Venue Hire Fees received by the Company pursuant to this Agreement.

(ii) The hire fee must be cleared in full 6 weeks before the proposed event date.

(iii) The Venue reserves the right of admission.

(iv) The Venue operates an ID scan on entry. All persons must provide a valid form of photographic identification to gain access. This should be communicated to the Promoter's guest where possible.

(v) The Venue operates a zero tolerance policy towards drugs. Anyone caught in the possession of drugs will be detained and handed over to the police.

(vi) The Venue operates a 'No Search, No Entry' policy.

(vii) No entry will be allowed to persons under the age of 18.

(viii) All production materials including but not limited to banners,
builds, inflatables, projections, films and slides must be approved. The venue also reserves the right to refuse items if they do not comply with Health & Safety standards

(ix) The Venue does not condone fly posting. The Venue will pass on any notices served as a result of The Promoter acting illegally when promoting their event

(x) The Venue shall not accept liability for any damage incurred to any production materials and reserves the right to remove said objects, should the Promoter fail to do so.

(xi) The Venue shall accept no responsibility for any injury to customers sustained whilst attending the event, save through negligence of the Venue or of its suppliers.

(xii) The Venue shall accept no responsibility for any items lost or stolen during the course of the event, set-up or strike.

(xiii) The Venue has full public liability and personal injury insurance.

(xiv) Whilst every effort will be made to ensure the provision of the facilities detailed, the Venue cannot be held responsible for shortcomings or conditions which may affect the event and which are outside its control (e.g. weather, acts of terrorism, fire etc).

(xv) The cash machine and credit card machines in the venue are used at the management's discretion.

(xvi) The Venue reserve the right to operate the venue split (i.e. one party using one red room / one party using black room) if The Hirer is not utilizing the whole venue for their event. This may result in shared toilet / smoking facilities. The venue will inform the promoter of this in advance of the event.

4. Agreement

This agreement contains all its terms and conditions as witnessed by the signature of the parties hereunder and initials of the said parties on each page.

On Behalf of the Venue
Name:        Signature:              Date:

On Behalf of Promoter:
Name:        Signature:              Date:

##### – – – – –Sample Talent Agreement– – – – –

Presenter and Artist Agreement
This agreement is made this _____ day of
_____, 20__ by and between _____ (Presenter)
_____ (hereinafter referred to as the "Presenter")
and _____ Artist_____ , if more than one, listed on
Addendum A attached hereto and included herein
(hereinafter referred to as the "Artist"), by and through their
designated agent or representative ("Manager") identified
below.

WHEREAS, Presenter conducts the event known as:
_____
(hereinafter referred to as the "Performance "); and
_____Artist_____

WHEREAS, Presenter desires to hire Artist, as independent
contractor(s), to provide the Performance generally
described below (the "Performance").

WHEREAS, Artist(s) desire to provide such Performance;
The parties agree as follows:

1. Artists: The names and addresses of the Artist who will
appear during the Performance, the amounts to be paid to
each.

2. Agent/Manager: The name and mailing address of the
Representative, who is executing this Agreement on behalf
of                        Artist(s),                    is:
_____

3. Place of Performance: The place of performance is at
_____

4. Date(s) and Time(s) of Performance:
The date(s) of the Performance shall be
_____, 2002 and the time(s) of the
Performance shall be _____. This
Performance shall be _____ hours with a _____
intermission.

5. Performance: The Performance is generally described as:

_____

6. Agreement to Perform: Artist(s) agree to provide the Performance in accordance with the terms of this Agreement and any addendums or riders hereto.

7. Price of Performance: Presenter agrees to pay Artist or his agent an aggregate of _____ DOLLARS ($0000) for the Performance by cheque immediately following the Performance. The cheque shall be made payable                                                     to:

_____.

8. Recording, Reproduction or Transmission of Performance: Presenter will use its best efforts to prevent the recording, reproduction or transmission of the Performance without the written permission of Artist(s) or Artist's representative.

9. Excuse of Obligations: Presenter and Artist shall be excused from their obligations hereunder in the event of proven sickness, accident, riot, strike, epidemic, act of God or any other legitimate condition or occurrence beyond their respective control.

10. Taxes: Presenter agrees to prepare and file all tax information required of a person who hires an independent contractor and Artist(s) agree that they have sole

responsibility for the payment of any federal or provincial taxes arising from the monies paid by Presenter to Artist(s) for the Performance.

11. Indemnify for Copyright Infringement: Artist(s) represent and warrant that they are knowledgeable about the copyright laws of Canada as applicable to the Performance, and that Artist(s) shall not perform any copyrighted materials of others during Performance without full compliance with such applicable copyright laws. In the event that Artist(s) breach this representation, warranty and covenant, Artist(s) hereby agree to INDEMNIFY AND HOLD HARMLESS Presenter and its employees, guests and agents from and against all liability, loss, damages, claims, and expenses (including attorney's fees) arising out of such breach.

12. Independent Contractor: Artist(s) acknowledge that they shall perform their obligations hereunder as an independent contractor and not as an employee of Presenter. Artist(s) further acknowledge that they are not on Presenter's payroll and/or tax withholding rolls. Artist(s) shall have sole control and direction in the conduct of the Performance.

13. Merchandising: Artist(s) shall not sell any goods, products, merchandise or services (other than the services provided herein) at the performance except by express written permission of Presenter.

14. Promotion: Presenter shall be entitled to advertise and promote the appearance of Artist(s) and the Performance. Artist(s) acknowledge that Presenter will rely on the terms hereof in all such promotions and advertising and in the brochures to be printed setting forth the names, dates and times of all performances to be held. Artist(s) hereby

acknowledge and agree that Presenter may use their names, photographs, likeness, facsimile signature and any other promotional materials in all of such promotions, advertising or other activities used to increase attendance at performance.

15. Parking: Presenter shall provide parking space for vehicles in a location of close proximity to and with direct access to the backstage area where Performance will take place on the date(s) of Performance. This parking space will be reserved for Artist(s) for a period of four (4) hours prior to the Performance and ending three (3) hours following the Performance.

16. Security: Presenter shall provide security for the backstage and stage areas before, during and after the Performance. Presenter shall provide security personnel to protect Artist(s) and their property as deemed appropriate by Presenter in its discretion.

17. Passes: Presenter shall provide identification passes to Artist(s) for the backstage and stage where Performance is to be held.

18. Stage: At its sole expense, Presenter shall furnish the stage, and stage lighting, sound and power for the Performance, and Presenter shall provide all stagehands required to assist the setup for and conduct of the Performance and takedown after the Performance.

19. Dressing Rooms: Presenter shall provide Artist(s) with one private dressing room, which will be clean, dry, well-lit and air-conditioned.

20. Authority to Execute: The representative who is executing this Agreement on behalf of Artist(s) hereby warrants and represents that he has the full power and authority to bind Artist(s) on whose behalf he is executing this Agreement and acknowledges that he is making this representation and warranty with the understanding that Presenter is relying thereon.

In Witness Hereof, this Agreement is executed on the date first above written.

Presenter (Authorized signature)

By: _____

Date:_____

Artist/Agent or Manager representative

By: _____

Date:_____

─ ─ ─ ─ ─ ─Sample Offer Sheet─ ─ ─ ─ ─ ─ ─

**Artist**: BIG ARTIST
Show Date: Thursday Feb 9 2014 - doors open at 9pm

Offer/Fee: $11,000 CDN flat (plus taxes)
Radius Clause: 100km, 45 days before/45 days after show
Offer Expires: Tuesday Nov 22 2013, 5pm EST

**Venue Information:**
Name: Big Awesome Venue
Address: 123 Bar Street, Las Vegas NV        Contact: Louie La
Vella

**Purchaser Information:**
Name: La Vella Entertainment Group Inc
Contact: Louie La Vella        Phone: (905) 555-1234        Email:
louie@mypromo.com

**Tickets:**
Capacity: 850                Pricing - Advanced $25, General
Admission $30
Gross Potential: $21,250 (-2762.50 TAX) = $18,487.50
Available Online via ticketbreak.com and as printed tickets
at venue & retail outlets.

**Purchaser to Provide**
**Sound and Lights**: Yes, technical rider to be approved by
purchaser
Company: Niagara AV
Contact: Mike Lighting-Guy        Phone: (905) 555-2222
Email: av@emailus.com

Travel: N/A        MEALS: N/A
Accommodations: yes, 5 rooms (Mandelay Bay Las Vegas)

Hospitality: Yes, green room rider to be approved by purchaser

Merchandise: 80% Artist/20% Purchaser (purchaser will provide table(s) and space)

Opening Act Support: $500 CDN (act to be mutually agreed upon)

*Offer is pending rider(s) approval by purchaser. Headlining artist and management agrees to support of the show in the following: allowing purchaser to prize or sell 10 VIP tickets (that include an autograph/picture meet and greet with artist. Conditions to be mutually agreed upon); and offer social media promotion of the show (via Facebook and twitter promoting the date and buy ticket URL).*

- - - - - - - - - - - - -

Signed by Purchaser - PROMOTER/BUYER

# — — —Sample Weekly Night Expenses— — —

**Artist: RAVE - SML ACT or THEME**

Date: OPEN
City: BIG CITY
Venue: VENUE Centre

| POTENTIAL SALES | | 3,000 | 2,500 | 2,000 | 1,500 |
|---|---|---|---|---|---|
| Early Bird Sales (20%) | 20.00 | $ 12,000.00 | $ 10,000.00 | $ 8,000.00 | $ 6,000.00 |
| Advanced Sales (30%) | 30.00 | $ 27,000.00 | $ 22,500.00 | $ 18,000.00 | $ 13,500.00 |
| General/Door (50%) | 40.00 | $ 60,000.00 | $ 50,000.00 | $ 40,000.00 | $ 22,500.00 |
| Gross Revenue | | $ 99,000.00 | $ 82,500.00 | $ 66,000.00 | $ 42,000.00 |
| HST | | $ 12,870.00 | $ 10,725.00 | $ 8,580.00 | $ 5,460.00 |
| Net Revenue | | $ 86,130.00 | $ 71,775.00 | $ 57,420.00 | $ 36,540.00 |
| Bar Revenue | $10/head | $ 30,000.00 | $ 25,000.00 | $ 20,000.00 | $ 15,000.00 |

**Fixed Expenses**

| | | | | | |
|---|---|---|---|---|---|
| ARTIST GUARANTEE | | $ 7,000.00 | $ 7,000.00 | $ 7,000.00 | $ 7,000.00 |
| CDN Work Permit | | $ 450.00 | $ 450.00 | $ 450.00 | $ 450.00 |
| Opening Act(s) | | $ 1,000.00 | $ 1,000.00 | $ 1,000.00 | $ 1,000.00 |
| Accommodations (up to 6 rooms) | | $ 800.00 | $ 800.00 | $ 800.00 | $ 800.00 |
| Producer Fee | | $ 2,000.00 | $ 2,000.00 | $ 2,000.00 | $ 2,000.00 |
| Producer Bonus ($1 per ticket sold) | | $ 3,000.00 | $ 2,500.00 | $ 2,000.00 | $ 1,500.00 |
| Box Office/Door Staff | | $ 100.00 | $ 100.00 | $ 100.00 | $ 100.00 |
| Green Room and/or Meals | | $ 200.00 | $ 200.00 | $ 200.00 | $ 200.00 |
| Travel (Ground or Buy Out) | | $ 500.00 | $ 500.00 | $ 500.00 | $ 500.00 |
| Security (20 guards) | | $ 4,000.00 | $ 4,000.00 | $ 4,000.00 | $ 4,000.00 |
| Technical Rider Stage/Sound/Lights | | $ 7,500.00 | $ 7,500.00 | $ 7,500.00 | $ 7,500.00 |
| Venue Rental | | $ 10,000.00 | $ 10,000.00 | $ 10,000.00 | $ 10,000.00 |
| Radio Advertising | | $ 2,000.00 | $ 2,000.00 | $ 2,000.00 | $ 2,000.00 |
| Social Media Ads | | $ 500.00 | $ 500.00 | $ 500.00 | $ 500.00 |
| Ticket Printing | | $ 150.00 | $ 150.00 | $ 150.00 | $ 150.00 |
| Tix Sellers Commissions ($5/tix selling 25%) | | $ 3,750.00 | $ 3,125.00 | $ 2,500.00 | $ 1,875.00 |
| Posters/Flyers | | $ 100.00 | $ 100.00 | $ 100.00 | $ 100.00 |
| Banners and Signage | | $ 200.00 | $ 200.00 | $ 200.00 | $ 200.00 |
| BAR expenses (staff tables etc) | | $ 3,000.00 | $ 3,000.00 | $ 3,000.00 | $ 3,000.00 |
| Barracades | | $ 1,000.00 | $ 1,000.00 | $ 1,000.00 | $ 1,000.00 |
| Miscellaneous | | $ 500.00 | $ 500.00 | $ 500.00 | $ 500.00 |

| | | | | | |
|---|---|---|---|---|---|
| Show Cost | | $ 47,750.00 | $ 46,625.00 | $ 45,500.00 | $ 44,375.00 |
| Potential Investor Profits | | $ 38,380.00 | $ 25,150.00 | $ 11,920.00 | -$ 7,835.00 |
| Potential Bar Profits After Expenses (33%) | | $ 8,910.00 | $ 7,260.00 | $ 5,610.00 | $ 3,960.00 |
| AVG Split Point at Advanced Price | | 1,592 | 1,554 | 1,517 | 1,479 |

# APPENDIX B: USEFUL RESOURCES

Here are a few great online resources that I have used in building my nightlife marketing company.

While these are offered around the world and sometimes buying online is inexpensive for the most part, you definitely want to look at your local businesses as well and compare quality and price. Nothing beats working face to face with people and supporting your local economy.

Printing Services
www.eprintfast.com
www.vistaprint.com

SMS Text Message Marketing
www.tatango.com
www.eztexting.com
www.simpletexting.com

Virtual Phone Numbers
www.voip.ms
www.skype.com
www.twilio.com

Mobile App Building
www.seattleclouds.com
www.createcoolapps.com
www.ibuildapp.com

Email Marketing
www.mailchimp.com
www.constantcontact.com
www.aweber.com

Online Ticket Sales
www.ticketmaster.com
www.ticketweb.com
www.eventbrite.com
www.venuedriver.com
www.wanttickets.com

Ticket Printing Services
www.comtix.com
www.eprintfast.com
www.ticketweb.com

Domain Names
www.godaddy.com
www.1and1.com
www.netfirms.com

Web Hosting
www.godaddy.com
www.doteasy.com

Outsourcing Services
www.odesk.com
www.elance.com
www.textbroker.com
www.iwriter.com
www.fiverr.com

Social Media Scheduling and Automation
www.bufferapp.com

www.sproutsocial.com
www.hootsuite.com

Talent Agencies
www.wmeentertainment.com
www.amonly.com
www.spinartistagency.com
www.apa-agency.com
www.slfa.com
www.hrbooking.com
www.moodswing360.com
www.theagencygroup.com
www.windishagency.com

Bar and Nightlife Resources
www.louielavella.com
www.lavellanightlife.com
www.nightlifemarketingresource.com
www.nextbigsound.com
www.concertideas.com
www.nightclub.com

# ABOUT THE AUTHOR

Louie La Vella has been in the nightlife marketing industry for 20 years, and counting.

Starting out at the age of 17 he built a successful career from the promoter business to concert producer to nightclub and bar marketing consultant.

The experience gained during these years have been extremely valuable and profitable to ownership, management and event producers combined.

Recent Promoter of the Year recipient, speaker in the industry and author of several books on nightlife marketing; which are available on Amazon, Kindle and local bookstores.

Louie was also a television host and producer for a national music channel in Canada, interviewing the likes of Lady Gaga, Richard Branson, Tommy Lee, Deadmau5 and more.

— / —

La Vella is a sought after consultant to the Nightclub and Bar industry for years. Working with clients from around the world to develop marketing initiatives, successful events and teach the tools of today's marketing landscape.

Contact Louie online at **www.louielavella.com** to schedule a Strategy Session and fast track your Nightlife Success.